Praise for other books

FreeBSD Mastery: ZFS

"Once again, a great FreeBSD book to read." — *Wendy Michele, nixCraft*

"ZFS Mastery covers what everyone using or administering these filesystems needs to know to work with them every day. It's fascinating to see how the system is used, having seen how it is implemented." — *George V. Neville-Neil, co-author of "Design and Implementation of the FreeBSD Operating System"*

Networking for Systems Administrators

"There is a lot of useful information packed into this book. I recommend it!" — *Sunday Morning Linux Review, episode 145*

After reading this book, you'll have a strong footing in networking. Lucas explains concepts in practical ways; he makes sure to teach tools in both Unix/Linux and Windows; and he gives you the terms you'll use to explain what you're seeing to the network folks. Along the way there's a lot of hard-won knowledge sprinkled throughout…" — *Slashdot*

FreeBSD Mastery: Specialty Filesystems

"a joy and treasure to read" — *Vivek Gite, nixCraft*

"I'm a fan of his books… he presents them in a way that makes them much more understandable. He has the right mix of humor and information." — *Sunday Morning Linux Review*

Sudo Mastery

"It's awesome, it's Lucas, it's sudo. Buy it now." — *Slashdot*

"Michael W Lucas has always been one of my favorite authors because he brings exceptional narrative to information that has the potential to be rather boring. Sudo Mastery is no exception." — *Chris Sanders, author of Practical Packet Analysis*

Absolute OpenBSD, 2nd Edition

"Michael Lucas has done it again." — *cryptednets.org*

"After 13 years of using OpenBSD, I learned something new and useful!" — *Peter Hessler, OpenBSD Journal*

"I doubt that a better book on OpenBSD could be written." — *Sandra Henry-Stocker, ITWorld.com*

"It quickly becomes clear that Michael actually uses OpenBSD and is not a hired gun with a set word count to satisfy... In short, this is not a drive-by book and you will not find any hand waving." - *Michael Dexter, callfortesting.org*

DNSSEC Mastery

"When Michael descends on a topic and produces a book, you can expect the result to contain loads of useful information, presented along with humor and real-life anecdotes so you will want to explore the topic in depth on your own systems." — *Peter Hansteen, author of The Book of PF*

"Pick up this book if you want an easy way to dive into DNSSEC." — *psybermonkey.net*

SSH Mastery

"...one of those technical books that you wouldn't keep on your bookshelf. It's one of the books that will have its bindings bent, and many pages bookmarked sitting near the keyboard." — *Steven K Hicks, SKH:TEC*

"...SSH Mastery is a title that Unix users and system administrators like myself will want to keep within reach..." — *Peter Hansteen, author of The Book of PF*

"This stripping-down of the usual tech-book explanations gives it the immediacy of extended documentation on the Internet. Not the multipage how-to articles used as vehicles for advertising, but an in-depth presentation from someone who used OpenSSH to do a number of things, and paid attention while doing it." — *DragonFlyBSD Digest*

Network Flow Analysis

"Combining a great writing style with lots of technical info, this book provides a learning experience that's both fun and interesting. Not too many technical books can claim that." — *;login: Magazine, October 2010*

"This book is worth its weight in gold, especially if you have to deal with a shoddy ISP who always blames things on your network." — *Utahcon.com*

"The book is a comparatively quick read and will come in handy when troubleshooting and analyzing network problems." —*Dr. Dobbs*

"Network Flow Analysis is a pick for any library strong in network administration and data management." — *Midwest Book Review*

FreeBSD Mastery: Storage Essentials

"If you're a FreeBSD (or Linux, or Unix) sysadmin, then you need this book; it has a lot of hard-won knowledge, and will save your butt more than you'll be comfortable admitting. If you've read anything else by Lucas, you also know we need him writing more books. Do the right thing and buy this now." — *Slashdot*

"If you are administering FreeBSD systems, especially ones that deal with dedicated storage, you will find this useful." — *DragonFlyBSD Digest*

Absolute FreeBSD, 2nd Edition

"I am happy to say that Michael Lucas is probably the best system administration author I've read." — *Richard Bejtlich, CSO, MANDIANT, and TaoSecurity blogger*

"Master practitioner Lucas organizes features and functions to make sense in the development environment, and so provides aid and comfort to new users, novices, and those with significant experience alike." — *SciTech Book News*

"...reads well as the author has a very conversational tone, while giving you more than enough information on the topic at hand. He drops in jokes and honest truths, as if you were talking to him in a bar." — *Technology and Me Blog*

Cisco Routers for the Desperate, 2nd Edition

"If only Cisco Routers for the Desperate had been on my bookshelf a few years ago! It would have definitely saved me many hours of searching for configuration help on my Cisco routers." — *Blogcritics Magazine*

"For me, reading this book was like having one of the guys in my company who lives and breathes Cisco sitting down with me for a day and explaining everything I need to know to handle problems or issues likely to come my way. There may be many additional things I could potentially learn about my Cisco switches, but likely few I'm likely to encounter in my environment." — *IT World*

"This really ought to be the book inside every Cisco Router box for the very slim chance things go goofy and help is needed 'right now.'" — *MacCompanion*

Absolute OpenBSD

"My current favorite is Absolute OpenBSD: Unix for the Practical Paranoid by Michael W. Lucas from No Starch Press. Anyone should be able to read this book, download OpenBSD, and get it running as quickly as possible." — *Infoworld*

"I recommend Absolute OpenBSD to all programmers and administrators working with the OpenBSD operating system (OS), or considering it." — *UnixReview*

"Absolute OpenBSD by Michael Lucas is a broad and mostly gentle introduction into the world of the OpenBSD operating system. It is sufficiently complete and deep to give someone new to OpenBSD a solid footing for doing real work and the mental tools for further exploration… The potentially boring topic of systems administration is made very readable and even fun by the light tone that Lucas uses." — *Chris Palmer, President, San Francisco OpenBSD Users Group*

PGP & GPG

"...unless you're a cryptographer, or never use email, you should read this book." — *Len Sassaman, CodeCon Founder*

Tarsnap Mastery

"If you use any nix-type system, and need offsite backups, then you need Tarsnap. If you want to use Tarsnap efficiently, you need Tarsnap Mastery." *–Sunday Morning Linux Review episode 148*

"This book is a great way to feel confident about backing up your data securely in cloud or through off-site backups, without compromising security or burning your pocket with enterprise grade products from IT vendors." — *Wendy Michele, nixCraft*

About Michael W Lucas

"The next Stephen Bourne." – *Peter Wemm, FreeBSD core team member and longest surviving FreeBSD cluster engineer*

"I hate you so much right now, Michael." – *George V. Neville-Neil, FreeBSD core team member and co-author of "The Design and Implementation of the FreeBSD Operating System," when Lucas gave him a perfectly innocent puzzle pen*

About Allan Jude

"Thanks for making ZFS *knowable* by everyone" – *Matt Ahrens, co-creator of ZFS*

"I'm sure he's thrilled beyond words to see the last of me." – *Michael W Lucas, co-author*

"Thank you for doing this… now I don't have to" – *Jeff Bonwick, co-creator of ZFS*

FreeBSD Mastery

Advanced ZFS

Allan Jude

Michael W Lucas

Tilted Windmill Press

FreeBSD Mastery: Advanced ZFS

Authors: Allan Jude, Michael W Lucas
Copyediting: Lindy Lou Losh
Cover art: Eddie Sharam, after Schwind's *Saint Wolfgang and the Devil.*

ISBN-13: 978-1-64235-001-2 (Tilted Windmill Press)
ISBN-10: 1-64235-001-X

Tilted Windmill Press
https://www.tiltedwindmillpress.com

FreeBSD Mastery

Advanced ZFS

Allan Jude

Michael W Lucas

Brief Contents

Complete Contents

Acknowledgements

Our gratitude goes to the people who offered feedback on the manuscript that became this book: Will Andrews, Marie Helene Kvello-Aune, Josh Paetzel, Benedict Reuschling, Alan Somers, Matthew Seaman, and Wim Wauters.

Lucas' portions of this book were largely written on hardware from iX Systems (http://www.ixsystems.com). He'd also like to thank his wife Liz for shoving food under his office door as he wrote this book.

The authors would like to thank the FreeBSD Project and the FreeBSD Foundation for providing access to NVMe devices in the NetPerf cluster, and to Sentex Data Communications for hosting said cluster. Lucas would like to thank Jude for somehow convincing these folks to grant Jude cluster access, because there's no way they'd give it to Lucas. Also because it means that Lucas didn't have to write that part of the book.

Chapter 0: Introduction

The Z File System, or ZFS, is a complicated beast, but it is also the most powerful tool in a sysadmin's Batman-esque utility belt. This book tries to demystify some of the magic that makes ZFS such a powerhouse, and give you solid, actionable intel as you battle your storage dragons.

ZFS contains over 100 "engineering years" of effort from some of the best minds in the industry. While it has competitors, such as B-Tree File System (BTRFS), those competitors have a lot of catching up to do. And ZFS races further ahead every day.

This book takes you into some of the more complicated and esoteric parts of managing ZFS. If you want to know why a single gigabyte of data fills your 2 GB drive, if you want to automatically update your disaster recovery facility, or if you just want to use boot environments on your laptop, *FreeBSD Mastery: Advanced ZFS* is for you.

Just about everything in this book applies in general to OpenZFS. We use FreeBSD as the reference platform, but the mechanics of using OpenZFS don't change much among platforms.

Prerequisites

The title of the book includes the word "Advanced." We expect you to know a couple things before you can use this. The easy answer would be that you should read and assimilate two earlier *FreeBSD Mastery* titles: *Storage Essentials* and *ZFS*. But you might already know what's in those books, so here are some details on what you need to bring with you.

You'll need familiarity with FreeBSD's storage management layer, GEOM. On non-FreeBSD platforms you can use disks and partition devices for ZFS. Always use ZFS on disk or partition devices, not on RAID or other software devices.

We assume you're familiar with ZFS pools and datasets. You know how to add VDEVs to a pool, and understand why you can't add a lone disk to your RAID-Z. You can take snapshots and create clones.

If you want to use FreeBSD's encrypted ZFS support, you must understand FreeBSD's GELI encryption. (You could use GBDE if you're relying on the encryption to preserve human life, but the built-in GELI support suffices for most of us. Also, GELI takes advantage of the AES-NI hardware crypto acceleration in modern CPUs.)

ZFS Best Practices

While you can acquire all the needed ZFS knowledge from publicly available documentation, that won't give you the ZFS best practices we've discussed in earlier books. As with so many other things in technology, the nice thing about best practices is that there are so many of them to choose from.

We're discussing some of our best practices here. Perhaps these practices are better than yours and you'll gleefully adopt them. Maybe they'll spark some improvements in your existing best practices. Even if your best practices blow ours away, these at least display our biases so you know how we're approaching the issues of storage management.

Space Management

With copy-on-write filesystems, deleting files uses space. Sysadmins accustomed to traditional filesystems might hear this when they start with ZFS, but don't really internalize it until the first time they run out of disk and suffer a nasty shock. As the pool approaches capacity, ZFS needs more and more time to store additional data blocks.

Performance degrades. While the ZFS developers keep reducing the performance impact of fragmentation, it becomes more and more of an issue as the pool approaches 100% utilization.

Recovering from a completely full pool is terribly hard. To prevent all of the space from being used, or to at least provide a warning ahead of time, create a *reservation.*

Ideally, you should create a reservation for 20% of the capacity of your pool. You can always lower the reservation to buy time while you work on adding more capacity or removing old data. The last thing you want is to unexpectedly run out of space. This can give you the soft landing that the Unix File System (UFS) offers, where only **root** can use up the last few percent of available disk space.

On this 1 TB pool, we create a new dataset with 200 GB refreservation.

```
# zfs create -o refreservation=200G mypool/reserved
```

Any time you're exploring space issues on a ZFS dataset, remember the `zfs get space` command. You'll see all of the space-related properties in a single convenient display.

```
# zfs get space zstore/usr
NAME         PROPERTY              VALUE         SOURCE
zstore/usr   name                  zstore/usr  -
zstore/usr   available             5.00T         -
zstore/usr   used                  367M          -
zstore/usr   usedbysnapshots       0             -
zstore/usr   usedbydataset         140K          -
zstore/usr   usedbyrefreservation  0             -
zstore/usr   usedbychildren        367M          -
```

While `zfs get space` won't free up space for you, it's the quickest path to finding out where all your space went.

Picking a VDEV Type

As discussed at length in *FreeBSD Mastery: ZFS*, selecting the correct VDEV type when creating your pool is the most important decision you make. It affects the performance of your pool, as well as the expansion possibilities.

A study by Pâris, Amer, Long, and Schwarz (http://arxiv.org/ftp/arxiv/papers/1501/1501.00513.pdf) found that to build a disk array that could survive for four years with no human interaction, required triple parity RAID. Double parity, even with an unlimited number of spares, cannot maintain 99.999% (five nines) reliability over a four-year period.

Combine this consideration with the hardware you have and your expected future storage needs.

The Importance of Labels

By labeling drives, you save your future self a lot of headache. Label your disks and partitions before adding them to a ZFS pool—or, indeed, using them in any way, for reasons we'll discuss through this section.

Take the case of an unfortunate friend of Jude's, who created a pool with raw device names. When a device failed, he rebooted before replacing the disk. His pool looked a little different than he expected.

```
# zpool status
pool: data
state: DEGRADED
status: One or more devices is currently being resilvered.  The
        pool will continue to function, possibly in a degraded
        state.
action: Wait for the resilver to complete.
 scan:  resilver in progress since Sat Apr 11 17:49:38 2015
        62.0M scanned out of 1.55T at 5.16M/s, 87h40m to go
        9.81M resilvered, 0.00% done

config:
NAME                       STATE     READ WRITE CKSUM
data                       DEGRADED     0     0     0
 mirror-0                  DEGRADED     0     0     0
  spare-0                  UNAVAIL      0     0     0
   5694975301095445325     FAULTED      0     0     0  was /dev/da1
  da7                      ONLINE       0     0   856  (resilvering)
  da14                     ONLINE       0     0     0
 mirror-1                  ONLINE       0     0     0
  da1                      ONLINE       0     0     0
  da13                     ONLINE       0     0     0
```

Originally, the pool had consisted of two mirrors: mirror-0 of da1 and da15, and mirror-1 of da2 and da14. Disk da1 failed.

FreeBSD dynamically assigns disk device nodes at boot. With da1 missing, FreeBSD numbered the remaining disk devices to shift one number lower. Disk da15 became da14, da14 became da13, and worst of all, da2 became da1.

So then mirror-1 contained da1—which was not the same da1 as the faulted disk. Mirror-0 was using its spare (da7) in place of what used to be called da1. Once Jude's unfortunate friend put a disk back in place for the failed da1, though, that da7 became da8.

ZFS doesn't use FreeBSD disk names to find the members of each VDEV, instead relying on its own on-disk label with a Globally Unique Identifier (GUID). ZFS can identify the disk no matter where the operating system puts its device node. And the operating system doesn't care either—it found the disk for you and mounted the filesystem; what more do you want?

This can easily confuse the human operator, though. Suddenly da1 is not the failed device, but a perfectly good device in another VDEV entirely! After the operator replaces the device and reboots the machine, the replaced drive will almost certainly become da1 again. All the device nodes will shift back to their original values. By the end of all of this, the sysadmin has no idea which disk is which. The only idea he'll have in mind is the need for a stiff drink.

Labeling Disks

FreeBSD provides several ways to label a disk or partition. Some are automatic, and some are managed by the user. Each has advantages and disadvantages. One device can have multiple labels.

Once a label is accessed, other label pointing at the same device wither and become inaccessible. This prevents accessing a single device by multiple names.

All of the automatically generated labels are activated by default. If you desire to use a manual label, it's best to disable the manual methods.

GPT Label (Manual)

If the disk is partitioned with a GUID Partition Table (GPT), each partition can contain a text label of your choosing. This is both authors' preferred method of labeling disks.

Use gpart(8) to create and label a new partition.

```
# gpart add -t freebsd-zfs -l zfs-mirror-1 da2
```

Here we change the label on the existing 2nd partition.

```
# gpart modify -i 2 -l f01-serialnum da2
```

Manual labels let you identify disks by characteristics such as physical placement or serial number.

If you use GPT labels, we recommend disabling GPTID and disk ID labels.

GPTID Label (Automatic)

With the GPT partitioning scheme, each partition has a unique GUID. The GPT ID labeling system uses the GUID to identify partitions. The problem is that GUIDs mean little to a human. By looking at a few examples, you can see that it can be hard to spot the differences.

```
ada0p1:  /dev/gptid/b305e4ff-b889-11e5-bace-002590db872e
ada1p1:  /dev/gptid/b329ff70-b889-11e5-bace-002590db872e
ada1p2:  /dev/gptid/b33db4ac-b889-11e5-bace-002590db872e
```

If only the last few characters of the first segment are actually different, it's easy to confuse yourself.

If ZFS sees a piece of a pool under a GPTID labels before seeing that same pool under a different label, it uses the GPTID label. This hides your carefully hand-crafted labels. Disable GPTID labels at boot by adding the following to */boot/loader.conf*.

```
kern.geom.label.gptid.enable=0
```

FreeBSD enables GPT ID labels by default.

Disk Ident Label (Automatic)

While GPT and GPTID labels identify a partition, the Disk Ident (or *diskid*) labels identify an entire disk. The device name is based on the disk's serial number, which is convenient. Unfortunately, any special characters in the serial number—notably, spaces—get encoded. This creates very ugly device names. In addition, since the label identifies the disk, not a partition, the partition part of the device name (p3) is appended, and can be hard to pick out of the device name.

```
/dev/diskid/DISK-07013121E6B2FA14
/dev/diskid/DISK-%20%20%20%20%20WD-WCC131365642
/dev/diskid/DISK-%20%20%20%20%20%20%20%20%20%20%20%20Z300HTCE
```

These autogenerated labels can be disabled to block ZFS from using them instead of your GPT label. Adding the following to */boot/loader.conf*:

```
kern.geom.label.disk_ident.enable=0
```

Many people have strong arguments in favor of diskid labels. The authors won't say those arguments are incorrect. We will say that diskid labels give both of us a headache.

FreeBSD enables diskid labels by default.

Glabel (Manual)

In addition to all the other types of labels, you can also create a GEOM label stored in the last sector of a disk or partition. These labels are in a GEOM-specific format, called *glabel*. The advantage to these custom glabels is that the do not require using the GPT format, so they can work with both MBR formatted disks and raw disks with no partitions. A glabel uses the provider's last sector.

Create and view glabels with glabel(8).

```
# glabel label -v mylabel /dev/ada0p2
Metadata value stored on /dev/ada0p2.
Done.
```

```
# glabel status
         Name  Status  Components
 gpt/gptboot0     N/A  ada0p1
label/mylabel     N/A  ada0p2
     gpt/zfs0     N/A  ada0p3
```

There is now a */dev/label/mylabel* device.

All labels must be unique. While you can apply the same label to multiple disks, only one shows up.

DTrace

Higher-level tuning of some ZFS features requires using DTrace, a program for tracing software behavior and performance.

Knowledgeably using DTrace with ZFS requires an understanding of the kernel internals. This is not a book on either DTrace or kernel internals. Grabbing an existing script and running it requires neither.

We would encourage you to use the output of these DTrace scripts both to solve your ZFS problems, and as entry points for choosing to learn about kernel internals. You might not need to be a programmer, but a professional sysadmin should develop understanding of how the system works.

Blindly running scripts is exactly the sort of "occult IT" that Lucas rants and rails against. That said, here's exactly how you blindly run a DTrace script.

DTrace uses kernel modules for the software probes that watch how software behaves: *dtrace.ko* and *dtraceall.ko*. You can load these automatically at boot in *loader.conf*. If the kernel modules aren't found, the dtrace(1) program automatically loads them the first time you run it.

You must run `dtrace` as **`root`**.

Copy your script to a file. Then run `dtrace -s`, giving the script as an argument.

Hit CTRL-C to interrupt the script.

You can download all of the DTrace scripts given in this book from Lucas' GitHub repo, linked from zfsbook.com.

A FreeBSD sysadmin with an understanding of how the kernel works can solve problems more quickly and correctly. For an overview of ZFS' internals, grab the latest edition of *The Design and Implementation of the FreeBSD Operating System* (Addison-Wesley Professional, 2014).[1] Similarly, DTrace is a powerful tool well worth learning and understanding. We recommend Gregg's and Mauro's book *DTrace:*

---

1 Some of the authors of *TD&IotFOS* use our ZFS books to learn how to deploy the code they write, so it all evens out.

Dynamic Tracing in Oracle Solaris, Mac OS X, and FreeBSD (Prentice Hall, 2011).

Book Overview

Chapter 0 is this introduction.

Chapter 1, "Boot Environments," takes you through using ZFS snapshots to create Solaris-style boot environments. Boot environments let you painlessly revert changes such as upgrades. You can even have multiple versions of FreeBSD installed simultaneously. Once you've used boot environments, you'll wonder how you ever lived without them.

Chapter 2, "Delegation and Jails," covers ZFS' internal permissions scheme. ZFS can let the sysadmin give select users and groups privileges to perform operations that normally require `root` access, such as snapshots and cloning.

Chapter 3, "Sharing Datasets," covers ZFS' network file sharing features. FreeBSD's ZFS is integrated with the Network File System, and is terribly useful for iSCSI devices.

Chapter 4, "Replication," teaches you how to replicate ZFS datasets to other machines. Replication can let you pick up a massive amount of data and ship it across the country or around the planet, and keep it up to date, without your users even noticing.

Chapter 5, "ZFS Volumes," discusses some fine details of creating and using block devices on top of a ZFS pool.

Chapter 6, "Advanced Hardware," is for the people who have really large storage arrays. If the words "SCSI multipathing" throw fear into your heart, or if you have no idea what NVMe is, this chapter is for you.

Chapter 7, "Caches," covers all of the various caching mechanisms. You'll learn about the Advanced Replacement Cache and all its variants, reading and writing caches, and the on-disk pool cache.

Chapter 8, "Performance," delves deep into how ZFS performs in different environments and how to determineif system changes might improve performance.

Chapter 9, "Tuning," discusses how to adjust ZFS to work best in your environment, hopefully without buying additional and more expensive hardware.

Finally, Chapter 10, "ZFS Potpourri," includes a bunch of short tips on using ZFS.

To those of you who read the introductions to books: congratulations. We hope you learned something, or were at least reminded of some important details. Let's go on to boot environments!

Chapter 1: Boot Environments

One of the most tediously terrifying system administration tasks is a system upgrade. We all know that the new kernel might not boot the system, but that's the least of your problems. What if a critical program requires an old version of a shared library? Maybe that new terminal mode is subtly incompatible with your software. Or perhaps your mission-critical software chokes on the new linker.

Things go wrong. Sometimes problems aren't apparent at first but only snarl at you after a week or two, when falling back becomes even more difficult. No matter what precautions you take or how much testing you perform, any upgrade can go bad.

We've developed all sorts of tools to work around bad upgrades. Boot loaders help you quickly recover from bad kernels. Backups help you slowly recover from bad userlands. But none of these help you understand exactly what went wrong and duplicate the problem.

Unless you're running ZFS, that is.

By combining snapshots and clones, you can create bootable backups of your operating system's kernel and userland. You want to upgrade? Clone your operating system datasets and go ahead. If the upgrade goes badly, boot the clone instead. This restores service while you use `zfs diff` to determine which files changed and which of them went wrong.

You can do all that by hand, but FreeBSD bundles this functionality into boot environments. With boot environment management tools, you can easily create, destroy, and deploy boot environments. Every time you're about to upgrade, create a new boot environment. If the upgrade goes bad, either immediately or even weeks later, you can revert to the old operating system version. The failed version stays around, so you can deploy it to another machine and study exactly what went wrong.

Using boot environments well requires that you understand how you've installed FreeBSD, however.

Installation Datasets

On FreeBSD 10.1 and newer, ZFS-based install creates datasets designed specifically for boot environments. These might seem counterintuitive at first glance. Take a look at a few of the datasets on a default install.

```
# zfs list
NAME                USED  AVAIL REFER  MOUNTPOINT
…
zroot/var           703K   188G  128K  /var
zroot/var/crash     128K   188G  128K  /var/crash
zroot/var/log       192K   188G  192K  /var/log
zroot/var/mail      128K   188G  128K  /var/mail
zroot/var/tmp       128K   188G  128K  /var/tmp
```

We have datasets for certain subdirectories of `/var`: `/var/crash`, `/var/log`, `/var/mail`, and `/var/tmp`. But what about all of the other directories under `/var`? The `/var/db` directory contains critical system information, like the package database. Surely that's at least as important as `/var/tmp`?

The default install doesn't create datasets based on the importance of the data in the directory. It creates datasets to separate data.

Now check `zfs mount` and see how these datasets are mounted.

```
# zfs mount
zroot/ROOT/default      /
...
zroot/var/crash         /var/crash
zroot/var/log           /var/log
zroot/var/mail          /var/mail
zroot/var/tmp           /var/tmp
```

Notice the missing dataset: */var*. That dataset exists, but isn't mounted (the `canmount` property is set to *no*). Files directly in */var* actually go in the dataset mounted as root, *zroot/ROOT/default*. Files under */var* that have their own dataset, such as */var/log/messages*, go in a separate dataset. Files that go under */var* but don't have their own dataset, such as */var/db*, go into the root dataset.

The location of data is critical to boot environments. Data likely to be affected by a boot environment goes on the root dataset. Data that you won't want to manage as part of the boot environment gets its own dataset.

Consider */var/db*. This contains critical information like the package database, the locate database, freebsd-update(8) records, and so on. All of this is tightly tied to the operating system version. Upgrading your host to a new operating system version requires using `freebsd-update`, and probably means updating your add-on software while you're at it. If you must revert an upgrade, you want these files reverted as well.

Compare that to */var/log*. If I must revert an upgrade, I specifically don't want my log files rolled back as well. Logs cover more than just the operating system. Similarly, home directories and the mail spool in */var/mail* had better not get rolled back with the operating system.[2]

---

2 We're told that the World Trade Organization considers tampering with a sysadmin's email to be grounds for execution. We haven't experimentally verified this, because it conforms to our prejudices.

FreeBSD upgrades affect specific directories. The core programs lurk in */bin*, */sbin*, */usr/bin*, and */usr/sbin*, with libraries in */lib* and */usr/lib*. Thanks to the non-mounting */usr* dataset, these directories are now on your root dataset. Packages install under */usr/local*, but it's also part of the root dataset. Similarly, thanks to the non-mounting */var*, the */var/db* directory with all that critical system information is also part of the root dataset.

Files that are not part of the core system, such as logs, user home directories, and so on, have their own datasets.

This segregates the core system and official packages from the rest of the host, letting you manage them as a single entity. The FreeBSD developers are working on packaging the base system as well as add-on packages, which might necessitate revisiting the system discussed here.

Using Boot Environments

ZFS' snapshot and clone functions let you save, copy, and duplicate filesystems. (We discussed snapshots and clones at length in *FreeBSD Mastery: ZFS*).

With ZFS, it's a good idea to snapshot datasets before performing system maintenance such as an upgrade. If the upgrade or change fails, you can roll back to the last known working version. To debug that failed upgrade, copy the snapshot onto a test system and debug it there, while your production system keeps chugging along on the slightly older operating system version.

A "boot environment" packages up pre-maintenance snapshots into a neat bundle, generally with a boot environment management program. You don't need a boot environment manager to use snapshots in system administration, but managers make maintaining all those snapshots much easier. FreeBSD has a boot environment manager, beadm(8), deliberately designed to resemble Solaris' beadm(8).

Install `beadm` with pkg(8).

```
# pkg install -y beadm
```

You're now ready to use boot environments.

Viewing Boot Environments

Each boot environment is a dataset under *zroot/ROOT*. A system where you've just installed `beadm` should have only one boot environment. Use `beadm list` to view all boot environments.

```
# beadm list
BE        Active  Mountpoint   Space   Created
default   NR      /            649.9M  2016-02-15 14:47
```

We have one environment, named *default*, after *zroot/ROOT/default*. This is a freshly installed system, so that's what you'd expect.

The *Active* column shows if this boot environment is in use. An *N* means that the environment is now running. An *R* means that the boot environment will be activated on reboot. The boot environment used at reboot comes from the pool's **bootfs** property.

The *Mountpoint* column shows the location of this boot environment's mount point. All live boot environments are normally mounted at `/`. If a boot environment is not in use, it normally isn't mounted and has the **canmount** property set to *off* or *noauto*. You could choose to mount an otherwise unused boot environment elsewhere.

The *Space* column shows the amount of disk space this dataset refers to.

The *Created* column shows the date this boot environment was created. In this case, it's the date the machine was installed.

Before changing the system, let's create a boot environment.

Creating Boot Environments

Name each boot environment after the existing install or environment. If you're creating a boot environment to prepare for upgrading packages, append the current date or some other identifying information. Use `freebsd-version` to check the FreeBSD version you're running.

```
# freebsd-version
10.3-RELEASE
```

Use `beadm create` to make a boot environment. Lucas is too lazy to hit caps lock, so the boot environment name is in all lower case.

```
# beadm create 10.3-release
Created successfully
```

We should now have two identical boot environments.

```
# beadm list
BE             Active  Mountpoint   Space  Created
default        NR      /           650.1M  2016-02-15 14:47
10.3-release   -       -           140.0K  2016-02-16 09:07
```

We're currently using the default boot environment, and this same boot environment will start on our next boot. The 10.3-release environment is available, however. At any time, you can tell FreeBSD to boot the 10.3-release environment and get the system as it was exactly when you created the environment.

The 10.3-release environment is very similar to the default environment. Note that it uses only 140 KB of space. That's enough to label a snapshot, but as we haven't made any changes to the filesystem yet, it takes up hardly any space.

Here I've run `freebsd-update` to update the environment to the latest patch level. The default boot environment gets the patches. The 10.3-release environment remains unchanged.

As you might expect, applying patches changes the boot environment's disk usage.

```
# beadm list
BE            Active  Mountpoint   Space Created
default       NR      /           650.1M  2016-02-15 14:47
10.3-release  -       -            69.7M  2016-02-16 09:07
```

The 10.3-release boot environment suddenly uses 69.7 MB of space. That's the space used by patches that have been applied between the 10.3-release boot environment and the current boot environment, 10.3-release-p13.

Activating Boot Environments

Suppose you apply the latest patches and the machine goes bonkers. Your server software fails, or the kernel panics, or tiny gremlins hop out of the USB ports and start stealing your spoons. Fall back to an earlier version by activating the boot environment and rebooting. Activate a boot environment with `beadm activate`.

```
# beadm activate 10.3-release
Activated successfully
# beadm list
BE             Active Mountpoint   Space  Created
default        N      /           308.1M  2015-06-19 10:04
10.3-release   R      -           457.1M  2015-06-19 14:13
```

The default boot environment has the Active flag set to *N*, meaning it's now running. The 10.3-release environment has the Active flag set to *R*, so after a reboot it will be live.

Reboot the system and suddenly you're back to running the 10.3-release boot environment, without any security updates and with whatever packages you originally installed on the system. You've fallen back to an older version of the operating system, with much less risk than restoring from backup.

Renaming Boot Environments

Sometimes you want to change the name of a boot environment. Maybe the name you picked wasn't as distinctive as you thought, or one of your minions thought to create a boot environment but named it *FeliciaGoesViking*. The `beadm rename` command lets you rename boot environments. Give two arguments: the original name and the new name.

This host has a boot environment called *install*. I'm changing that to be *10.3-release*, just like my other hosts.

```
# beadm rename install 10.3-release
Renamed successfully
```

This name is now consistent with the rest of my hosts.

Removing Boot Environments

If you create a whole bunch of boot environments, you'll start using more and more disk space. Some of these boot environments you'll never use again.

```
# beadm list
BE              Active Mountpoint  Space  Created
default         NR     /            3.6G  2015-04-28 11:53
install         -      -          126.0M  2015-04-28 12:19
10.3-p9         -      -          209.0M  2015-05-14 08:01
10.3-p10        -      -          169.0M  2015-05-24 11:02
10.3-p10-10Jun  -      -          150.0M  2015-06-10 14:24
10.3-p10-13Jun  -      -           47.3M  2015-06-13 06:19
10.3-p12        -      -            7.7M  2015-06-19 07:06
```

Using `freebsd-version` tells me this particular system is running FreeBSD 10.3-RELEASE-p13. It's conceivable that I might want to fall back to 10.3-p12. But I'm not going back to p10, or p9, or especially the install version. Eliminating these boot environments will save disk space and make my existing boot environments easier to read and understand.

Use `beadm destroy` and the boot environment name to remove unwanted boot environments.

```
# beadm destroy 10.3-release
Are you sure you want to destroy '10.3-release'?
This action cannot be undone (y/[n]): y
Destroyed successfully
```

My raw install of FreeBSD 10.3 is now gone from this system. Everything that remains is patched in one way or another. This will probably free up some space on the root pool—not all the space used by the boot environment, as snapshots and clones don't free space until the last snapshot that needs a block is destroyed. But you'll get some back.

Boot Environments and ZFS

Boot environments leverage ZFS snapshots and clones. But what exactly do they do? Look at the snapshots on the host we first installed.

```
# zfs list -t snapshot
NAME                                     USED  AVAIL  REFER  MOUNTPOINT
zroot/ROOT/default@2016-02-16-08:35:22 25.9M      -   479M  -
```

This host has one snapshot, named after the boot environment I created. The default boot environment is what's currently running, so it doesn't need a snapshot. Now look at the datasets under *zroot/ROOT*.

```
# zfs list -r zroot/ROOT
NAME                      USED  AVAIL  REFER  MOUNTPOINT
zroot/ROOT                765M   283G    96K  none
zroot/ROOT/10.3-release   457M   283G   457M  /
```

Each boot environment is a dataset under *zroot/ROOT*, cloned from the source snapshot. The boot environment default is *zroot/ROOT/default*, while the 10.3-release boot environment is at *zroot/ROOT/10.3-release*.

While all of the boot environment datasets have a `mountpoint` property of /, every boot environment dataset except the active one has `canmount` set to *off*. You can mount these datasets if you wish, but you'll want to specify a new mount point.

Destroying a boot environment destroys the associated snapshot and clone.

Accessing Unused Boot Environments

One way to access the contents of unused boot environments is to check the snapshots the boot environments were created from. The boot environments are accessible in the hidden */.zfs* directory. This is convenient for quick checks.

If you want to mount those boot environments read-write, use the `beadm mount` command and the boot environment name. The boot environment will be read-write mounted in a location under */tmp*.

```
# beadm mount 10.3-p19
Mounted successfully on '/tmp/BE-10.3-p19.DmtRWZGf'
```

When you finish with the environment, unmount it with `beadm umount`.

```
# beadm umount 10.3-p19
Unmounted successfully.
```

It is possible to mount and unmount boot environment snapshots with the `canmount` and `mountpoint` properties. If you do it incorrectly, however, you'll mount the old boot environment over the top of your running boot environment. While FreeBSD filesystems are stackable, changing all the system binaries on a running system can put you in a difficult situation. Imagine being unable to run reboot(8) because the binary can't talk to the running kernel!

Be safe. Use snapshot mounting and unmounting functions built into beadm(8).

Boot Environments at Boot

So you've truly hosed your operating system. Forget getting to multi-user mode—even single user mode has dissolved into a stream of error messages so obscure that even FreeBSD's most experienced kernel hackers think your hardware has been hitting the radiator booze. FreeBSD 10.3 and above lets you change your boot environment right at the loader prompt. This requires console access, but so would any other method of getting yourself out of this hole.

Boot the host. You'll get a loader menu much like this, plus some graphics.

```
+============Welcome to FreeBSD===========+
|                                         |
|  1. Boot Multi User [Enter]             |
|  2. Boot [S]ingle User                  |
|  3. [Esc]ape to loader prompt           |
|  4. Reboot                              |
|                                         |
|  Options:                               |
|  5. [K]ernel: kernel (1 of 2)           |
|  6. Configure Boot [O]ptions...         |
|  7. Select Boot [E]nvironment...        |
|                                         |
|                                         |
+=========================================+
```

Note item 7. Select it and you'll get a new menu.

```
+============Welcome to FreeBSD===========+
|                                         |
|  1. Active:                             |
|  2. bootfs: zfs:zroot/ROOT/default      |
|  3. [P]age: 1 of 1                      |
|                                         |
|  Boot Environments:                     |
|  4. 10.3-release                        |
|  5. default                             |
|                                         |
+=========================================+
```

Choose your preferred boot environment. The menu will update, displaying your chosen environment in space 1 (labeled *Active*). Press

`1` to go back to the main menu, or hit `ENTER` to boot. Your system will revert to a known working boot environment, giving you a chance to find out why everything went sideways.

Boot Environments and Applications

FreeBSD developed many traditional practices over the last decades, especially with add-on packages. Some of these are based on FreeBSD sensibilities: MySQL stashes data in */var/db/mysql*. Some are based on the software's preferences: PostgreSQL keeps its records in */usr/local/pgsql*. All of these pose possible problems when using boot environments.

Let's consider MySQL as an example. The directory */var/db/mysql* is part of the root dataset. It's included in boot environments. If you store your database data in a boot environment, falling back to an older boot environment will also revert your database data to an earlier version. This probably isn't what you want.

Other server software has exactly the same problem.

Dealing with this isn't hard, but it requires that you know your software. You have two choices: changing the application data location, or creating datasets in the old application directory. Both work fine once you understand your needs.

Moving Application Data

Moving application data requires creating a dataset for application data, and telling the application to use that location. Here, I decide to put my MySQL data in */var/mysql*.

```
# zfs create zroot/var/mysql
```

I now have to tell MySQL to use this data directory. Checking the variables in */usr/local/etc/rc.d/mysql-server* tells me I want the `mysql_dbdir` option in */etc/rc.conf*.

```
mysql_dbdir="/var/mysql"
```

I must move any existing data and configuration files from */var/db/mysql* to */var/mysql*, then restart the server.

Creating New Datasets

A boot environment affects only the root filesystem dataset. If you want to leave application data in the usual locations, you must create a new dataset for that data. Let's consider PostgreSQL as an example. PostgreSQL stores its data in */usr/local/pgsql*, so you could just create that dataset.

```
# zfs create zroot/usr/local/pgsql
cannot create 'zroot/usr/local/pgsql': parent does not
exist
```

Without a */usr/local* dataset, you cannot create *zroot/usr/local/pgsql*. But if you create a standard */usr/local* dataset, you'll either pull the files in */usr/local* out of the boot environment, or overlay an empty filesystem on top of the populated */usr/local* directory. As with */usr*, the solution is to create a filesystem with the **canmount** property set to *off*, and then create the child dataset.

```
# zfs create -o canmount=off zroot/usr/local
# zfs create zroot/usr/local/pgsql
```

You now have */usr/local/pgsql* as its own dataset, and can safely run PostgreSQL with boot environments.

Neither solution addresses messy software packages like Apache. Apache 2.4, for example, sticks lots of stuff in */usr/local/www* and */usr/local/etc/apache24*. The sysadmin is supposed to edit some, but not all, of those files. This complicates separation by ZFS datasets. For Apache and programs like it, I normally create an entirely new dataset, such as */var/www*, and put the active web site files there.

Disk Encryption and Boot Environments

The standard `beadm` boot environment manager only works with a single root filesystem dataset. A FreeBSD installation to a GELI-encrypted disk is incompatible with `beadm`.

Installing default FreeBSD with ZFS onto an encrypted disk device requires a small, unencrypted partition to store the boot kernel. The default installer creates the pool *bootpool* for this, and puts the */boot* in *bootpool/boot*. On a running system, */boot* is a symlink to this other pool. The rest of the system goes in the *zroot* pool.

You can use boot environments on encrypted disks. You just don't get the convenience of a boot environment manager. Take a snapshot before you upgrade your system. Clone that snapshot to create the old environment. Keep a copy of your kernel for each boot environment. Change which environment FreeBSD uses as the root filesystem with the *zroot* pool's **bootfs** property.

Booting the kernel requires a whole different process, however. Before patching your kernel you must create a copy of that kernel named after your boot environment. Before upgrading from, say, 10.3-RELEASE to 10.3-p5, you'll want to copy the 10.3-RELEASE kernel from */boot/kernel* to */boot/kernel.10.3R*. If you have to revert the boot environment, choose the old kernel at the loader menu.

PC-BSD 10 does support using boot environments on GELI-encrypted disks, but they use the GRUB boot loader and some special trickery.

FreeBSD 11.0 is expected to support booting from GELI encrypted ZFS without the separate *bootpool*, allowing boot environments to work the same as they do on unencrypted disks. That feature has not landed as of this book's publication date.

For most FreeBSD ZFS users, boot environments save a lot of trouble. Let's go on and talk about other ways to save you trouble.

Chapter 2: Delegation and Jails

The ZFS designers did their best to ease storage management for system administrators. One of the best ways to reduce the amount of work you do is to make someone else do the work for you. ZFS has a fully featured delegation system that lets you dictate what commands and features a user or group of users can use on each dataset. You can allow users to create and destroy their own snapshots, create child datasets, generate space consumption reports, or control the properties of a dataset. ZFS builds on the delegation feature to provide special support to jails.

ZFS Delegation

ZFS lets you delegate administrative tasks to users on a per-property and per-command basis for each dataset. You could give the database administrator complete control over the database pool, or the web server admin control over snapshots on the web site dataset. Use the `zfs allow` command to delegate permissions.

Giving `zfs allow` a pool or dataset as an argument shows the permissions on that device. Here I get the permissions on the pool *remotepool*.

```
# zfs allow remotepool
---- Permissions on remotepool -------------------------
Local+Descendent permissions:
     user replicator compression,create,destroy,mount,
mountpoint,receive
```

This pool has a single permission entry, for the user **replicator**. This user has rights to the **compression** and **mountpoint** properties, as well as the `create`, `destroy`, `mount`, and `receive` subcommands of `zfs`. (Chapter 4 discusses the importance of these particular permissions.)

Applications and users can define their own properties. Programs like `zfstools` create properties to manage snapshots. There is also a special permission, **`userprop`**, to allow users to create user-defined properties. User-defined properties are assigned as a single permission: you cannot separately assign different user-defined properties.

While **`root`** is not listed as having any permissions here, **`root`** can do whatever it dang well pleases. Because that's how Unix rolls.

Adding Permissions

Delegate permissions on a pool or a dataset to a user or group. The `-u` flag lets you specify a username to `zfs allow`, and `-g` specifies a group.

```
# zfs allow -u username permissions pool/dataset
```

Suppose we have a troublesome user—call him Lucas[3]. He keeps trying stupid Unix tricks that fry his home directory. Let's allow Lucas to create his own snapshots so he doesn't have to bother the sysadmin every time he breaks his environment.

```
# zfs allow -u lucas snapshot,rollback \
      mypool/usr/home/lucas
```

When you view the dataset permissions, the two permissions you've assigned show up.

```
# zfs allow mypool/usr/home/lucas
---- Permissions on mypool/usr/home/lucas -------------
Local+Descendent permissions:
     user lucas rollback,snapshot
```

Delegations are automatically inherited. When Lucas gained the ability to snapshot his home directory dataset, he also gained that permission on all of the child datasets of his home directory. For some reason he has a dataset called *`blackmail`*. It's probably where he stashes

3 I'm *certain* that when Jude wrote this section, he was thinking of some Lucas other than me. ==mwl

all of the photos and recordings he uses to get BSD developers to help him with research and technical reviews.[4]

```
# zfs allow mypool/usr/home/lucas/blackmail
---- Permissions on mypool/usr/home/lucas -------------
Local+Descendent permissions:
     user lucas rollback,snapshot
```

Lucas should have the access to create a snapshot. Before telling him it works, though, impersonate Lucas and create a snapshot.

```
# su lucas
$ zfs snapshot \
mypool/usr/home/lucas/blackmail@bsdcan_drunken_escapades
$ zfs list -t all -r -o name mypool/usr/home/lucas
NAME
mypool/usr/home/lucas
mypool/usr/home/lucas/blackmail
mypool/usr/home/lucas/blackmail@bsdcan_drunken_escapades
```

We know this works. Let's get rid of the snapshot before Lucas gets any ideas he doesn't already have.

```
$ zfs destroy \
mypool/usr/home/lucas/blackmail@bsdcan_drunken_escapades
cannot destroy snapshots: permission denied
```

Creating new datasets involves mounting them, and destroying a dataset obviously should include unmounting that. To be useful the `clone`, `create`, and `destroy` commands all require the **`mount`** permission. To grant **`lucas`** permissions, run `zfs allow -u lucas` and list the desired permissions and dataset.

```
# zfs allow -u lucas destroy,mount mypool/usr/home/lucas
```

Checking your work now shows every privilege you've assigned in both runs of `zfs allow`.

---

4 Not *all* of that material. And *definitely* some other Lucas. ==mwl

```
# zfs allow mypool/usr/home/lucas
---- Permissions on mypool/usr/home/lucas -------------
Local+Descendent permissions:
     user lucas destroy,mount,rollback,snapshot
```

Lucas can now shoot himself in the foot by destroying the dataset his home directory resides on. And he'll certainly call to whinge about it.

You can give a user permission to create and mount a dataset, but the operating system also has its say here. FreeBSD uses the sysctl vfs.usermount to determine if users can mount partitions. Set this sysctl to *1* to allow a user to mount partitions.

Even with that sysctl, allowing a regular user to mount filesystems comes with a safety belt that blocks users from doing evil things. A user must own the directory where he wants to mount anything. This prevents users from mounting their new dataset as */etc* and hijacking your system. The dataset might have restrictive permissions on it, but a user who owns the mount point and has the **mount** privilege can mount it.

To allow the regular user **lucas** to create, clone, and mount datasets under his home directory, set the sysctl and make sure he owns the directory you're letting him control.

```
# sysctl vfs.usermount=1
# zfs allow -u lucas create,clone,mount \
      mypool/usr/home/lucas
```

Log in as **lucas** again to verify it works.

```
# su lucas
$ zfs create mypool/usr/home/lucas/evil_plot
$ zfs mount
mypool/ROOT/default                /
...
mypool/usr/home                    /usr/home
mypool/usr/home/lucas              /usr/home/lucas
mypool/usr/home/lucas/blackmail    /usr/home/lucas/blackmail
mypool/usr/home/lucas/evil_plot    /usr/home/lucas/evil_plot
```

Remember to add `vfs.usermount=1` to your */etc/sysctl.conf* so he can still mount datasets after a reboot, or he'll come whining to you.

Revoking Permission

Giving permissions (and work) away to other people can be freeing, but nothing matches the feeling of taking permission away. Use `zfs unallow` to remove permissions from a dataset. The command follows the exact same syntax as `zfs allow`.

Here, user **lucas** has created too many children and we decide he should not longer be allowed to procreate. Get rid of his `create` permission.

```
# zfs unallow -u lucas create mypool/usr/home/lucas
# zfs allow mypool/usr/home/lucas
---- Permissions on mypool/usr/home/lucas -------------
Local+Descendent permissions:
     user lucas clone,destroy,mount,rollback,snapshot
```

Permissions can also be removed recursively, with the `-r` flag, which makes sure the permission is removed even from distant child datasets where you might have manually set a privilege.

Delegation Inheritance

ZFS' delegated permissions are automatically inherited. If you give a user privileges over *zroot/db*, she automatically gets those same privileges over all children of *zroot/db*. The `zfs allow` subcommand can also restrict permission inheritance. Inherited permissions can be local, or apply to descendents.

Local permissions apply only to the specified dataset. We might allow **lucas** permissions to snapshot *zroot/usr/home/lucas*, but not snapshot the child datasets. He'll have to manage his blackmail material the old-fashioned way. Set privileges to be local only with the `-l` flag.

```
# zfs allow -lu lucas clone,destroy,mount,rollback,
snapshot zroot/home/lucas
```

The permissions now show up as local only, rather than local and descendent.

```
# zfs allow zroot/home/lucas
---- Permissions on zroot/home/lucas -------------------
Local permissions:
     user lucas clone,destroy,mount,rollback,snapshot
```

You can also apply permissions only to child datasets, and not the dataset in the command. The `-d` flag tells `zfs allow` that the permission applies only to the descendent datasets, not the parent on which the permissions were created. This can be used to allow users to destroy child datasets, but not the parent.

Here I want to allow **lucas** to destroy the snapshots he created, but not destroy his entire home directory. I use `-d` to specify that these permissions apply only to his home directory's child datasets, and not the home directory itself. I leave permissions for the `snapshot` and `rollback` commands in place on his home directory, so he can rescue himself if he doesn't screw up too badly.

```
# zfs allow -d lucas destroy,mount mypool/usr/home/lucas
# zfs allow mypool/usr/home/lucas
---- Permissions on mypool/usr/home/lucas -------------
Descendent permissions:
     user lucas destroy,mount
Local+Descendent permissions:
     user lucas rollback,snapshot
```

Once again, impersonate Lucas and test the permissions.

```
$ zfs destroy -v mypool/usr/home/lucas/desc
will destroy mypool/usr/home/lucas/desc
$ zfs destroy -v mypool/usr/home/lucas
cannot unmount '/home/lucas': Operation not permitted
```

Running `zfs destroy` on Lucas' home directory is now a pleasure reserved for the sysadmin.

Create Time Permissions

ZFS allows you to create permissions today, for datasets that won't exist until next Tuesday, or some other future time. *Create time* permissions apply to the user who creates a dataset. They're like a "sticky bit" for delegation. Define create time permissions with `-c`.

A common desire for these kinds of permissions is to give the permissions to everyone, rather than specifying every user on the system or defining a group that includes all users. Rather than `-u` or `-g` and a user or group name, use the `-e` flag to indicate everyone (all users).

Using create time permissions requires careful control of inheritance. You want the create time permissions to apply to child datasets, not the parent. The parent dataset should have its own privileges, set with `-l`.

Suppose we have a scratch dataset, usable by everyone. It's like a */tmp*, but with ZFS features. We want everyone to be able to create and mount datasets in this space, but not have access to trash the dataset as a whole. Those permissions must be restricted (via the `-l` flag) to that dataset, and not automatically inherited by the new children.

```
# zfs allow -l -e create,mount mypool/scratch
```

Now use `-c` to specify create time permissions assigned to newly created datasets.

```
# zfs allow -c snapshot,rollback,destroy mypool/scratch
```

Checking your work will show the create time permissions as permission sets.

```
# zfs allow mypool/scratch
---- Permissions on mypool/scratch ---------------------
Permission sets:
     destroy,rollback,snapshot
Local permissions:
     everyone create,mount
```

The real test is running these commands as a normal user, of course. Let's get **lucas** to create some datasets under *mypool/scratch*.

```
# su lucas
$ zfs create mypool/scratch/lucas
```

That worked. But what privileges does he have?

```
$ zfs allow mypool/scratch/lucas
---- Permissions on mypool/scratch/lucas --------------
Local permissions:
     user lucas destroy,rollback,snapshot
---- Permissions on mypool/scratch --------------------
Permission sets:
     destroy,rollback,snapshot
Local permissions:
     everyone create,mount
```

Now **lucas**, and only **lucas**, can create snapshots of and destroy his dataset. Other users can create their own datasets that only they have access to.

Permission to change permissions

A user with access to the `allow` command can delegate any other permissions that he already has. This lets you give a team leader or project manager the ability to take charge of permissions for his crew.

Consider the previous example of a scratch dataset. Suppose **lucas** wants to allow the **liz** user to create snapshots on his new scratch dataset.

First, give **lucas** the ability to delegate permissions by allowing him the `zfs allow` command.

```
# zfs allow -u lucas allow mypool/scratch/lucas
# zfs allow mypool/scratch/lucas
---- Permissions on mypool/scratch/lucas ---------------
Local permissions:
     user lucas destroy,snapshot
Local+Descendent permissions:
     user lucas allow
---- Permissions on mypool/scratch ---------------------
Permission sets:
     destroy,snapshot
Local permissions:
     everyone create,mount
```

Lucas can now delegate any permission he has to the **liz** account. Test this by logging in as him.

```
# su lucas
$ zfs allow -u liz snapshot mypool/scratch/lucas
$ zfs allow mypool/scratch/lucas
---- Permissions on mypool/scratch/lucas ---------------
Local permissions:
     user lucas destroy,snapshot
Local+Descendent permissions:
     user lucas allow
     user liz snapshot
---- Permissions on mypool/scratch ---------------------
Permission sets:
     destroy,snapshot
Local permissions:
     everyone create,mount
```

But Lucas can't give away permissions he does not have:

```
$ zfs allow -u liz clone mypool/scratch/lucas
cannot set permissions on 'mypool/scratch/lucas':
permission denied
```

The sysadmin can delegate permissions to a user, and make the user responsible for further delegation of his own dataset.

Permission Sets

Running `zfs allow` presents a list of over 60 permissions you can grant a user. We won't list them all here, but you can grant access to each zfs(8) subcommand and each pool and dataset property individually.

Rather than having to grant a long list of permissions to each user, and inevitably forgetting one, ZFS allows you to define sets of permissions. Use the `-s` flag and give a permission set name, beginning with the `@` sign. Then list the permissions in that set, and the name of the dataset that permission set is valid for.

```
# zfs allow -s @permissionset \
      permission,permission,permission… dataset
```

Here we create a permission set called *@dataset* that includes the permissions needed to manage datasets. It applies to the *mypool/teams* dataset.

```
# zfs allow -s @dataset create,destroy,mount,rename,
snapshot,rollback,clone,promote,hold,release \
      mypool/teams
```

Here's a permission set called *@replication* that offers the privileges needed for replication on that same dataset.

```
# zfs allow -s @replication send,receive mypool/teams
```

The *@billing* permission set grants access to the normally inaccessible **userused** and **groupused** properties on this dataset.

```
# zfs allow -s @billing userused,groupused mypool/teams
```

Here's a *@quotas* permission set that lets someone manage dataset space quotas.

```
# zfs allow -s @quotas userquota,groupquota,quota,
refquota,reservation,refreservation mypool/teams
```

Finally, here's a permissions set to let people adjust some basic dataset properties. Presumably the sysadmin sets these to reasonable defaults, but users might have specific datasets with special requirements.

```
# zfs allow -s @basic_properties compression,copies,
atime,primarycache,secondarycache mypool/teams
```

Once you establish permission sets, you can assign them to users and groups. Here, the managers group gets access to privileges in the *@dataset* and *@basic_properties* sets in their dataset.

```
# zfs allow -g managers @dataset,@basic_properties \
     mypool/teams
```

And here, we allow the **billbot** user that runs the billing system access to the billing permissions set on `mypool/teams`.

```
# zfs allow -u billbot @billing mypool/teams
```

Running `zfs allow` shows you the permission sets and the assigned permissions on a dataset.

```
# zfs allow mypool/teams
---- Permissions on mypool/teams ----------------------
Permission sets:
     @basic_properties atime,compression,copies,
primarycache,secondarycache
     @billing groupused,userused
     @dataset clone,create,destroy,hold,mount,promote,
release,rename,rollback,snapshot
     @quotas groupquota,quota,refquota,refreservation,
reservation,userquota
     @replication receive,send
Local+Descendent permissions:
     user billbot @billing
     group managers @basic_properties,@dataset
```

ZFS delegation can quickly become complex. As with many other permissions schemes, using groups can help simplify management. Assign permissions only when they're needed, not because you think you know how the system will evolve.

Delegation and Jails

FreeBSD supports a lightweight virtualization method called *jails*. You'll find many tutorials on using jails, so we won't get into the complexities of jails.[5] FreeBSD's ZFS implementation has special support for jails.

A dataset can be marked for use only in a jail. The jail's **root** user has full control of the dataset. She can create child datasets and change any properties she wishes.

A jailed dataset cannot be mounted on the host system. The jail dataset is untrusted, and might have property settings that are incompatible with—or actively hostile to—the host. As an easy example, the jail might have a dataset with a **mountpoint** of */etc*. Remember, BSD filesystems are stackable. If the host mounts that jail dataset, the jail's */etc* would stack over the host's */etc*. The host would suddenly have the jail's */etc/password*, *rc.conf*, *sshd_config*, and other vital system files. Worst case, the jail's sysadmin could claim control of the host. Best case, the host's sysadmin would have a really unhappy day.

As far as the jail's **root** user can tell, he almost completely controls the dataset. The only property he cannot change is the quota. Editing the quota might give him more access than the sysadmin allocated to him.

The jailed **root** account can see that it exists within a jail, however. The **root** account can see each of their dataset's parent datasets up to the root of the pool. If you have a *jails* pool and a jail exists in, say, *jails/customers/lucas*, the **root** user can see that path. They can't see any other datasets outside the jail, however. Other customer datasets are invisible.

5 Lucas keeps insisting that he's going to write a "jails mastery" book. Sadly, the storage books are somewhere between prequels and prerequisites.

Jailing a Dataset

To jail a dataset, set the `jailed` property to *on*. The host will no longer be able to mount the dataset.

To build a jail for Lucas, create a new dataset to serve as the root of his prison. Here we use the *zroot/jails/lucas/jail* dataset for the jail.

```
# zfs create -o jailed=on -o mountpoint=/jail \
      zroot/jails/lucas/jail
```

Once you have the dataset, start a temporary jail rooted in that dataset.

```
# jail -c path=/zroot/jails/lucas mount.devfs \
allow.mount allow.mount.zfs host.hostname=lucas \
ip4.addr="lo0|127.0.0.2" exec.poststart = \
"/sbin/zfs jail lucas zroot/jails/lucas/jail" \
command=/bin/sh
```

Now enter the jail.

```
# jexec lucas sh
```

As we're in the jail, we can create a new dataset.

```
jail# zfs create zroot/jails/lucas/jail/foo
```

The new dataset, and the jail's parent datasets, are visible.

```
jail# zfs list -o name,mountpoint
NAME                         MOUNTPOINT
zroot                        /zroot
zroot/jails                  /zroot/jails
zroot/jails/lucas            /zroot/jails/lucas
zroot/jails/lucas/jail       /jail
zroot/jails/lucas/jail/foo   /jail/foo
```

Are there other datasets in *zroot/jails* or, indeed, in the host underlying this jail? Users in the jail will never know.

The user **lucas** can now set mount points, create and destroy datasets, delegate datasets to regular users inside the jail, and so on. If only it were that easy to keep Lucas users from breaking things in the real world…

Building a ZFS Delegation Jail

Your jail users probably don't want a bare-bones jail as demonstrated above. They probably want an actual userland, with programs and the ability to run services. That means installing FreeBSD on your jailed dataset. Jails can be incredibly complex, so we won't completely cover them here. We'll do a basic FreeBSD install on a jailed dataset, so you can add ZFS to your existing jail processes.

First, create the jail dataset.

```
# zfs create -p mypool/jails/lucas/zroot
```

Now install the operating system on that dataset. You can install directly from the FTP site, as we do here with the amd64 version of FreeBSD 10.3.

```
# fetch -o - ftp://ftp.freebsd.org/pub/FreeBSD/
releases/amd64/10.3-RELEASE/base.txz | \
      tar -xJf - -C /mypool/jails/lucas/
```

If you intend to install multiple jails, download the *base.txz* for your version and extract it in each jail.

```
# tar -xf base.txz -C /mypool/jails/lucas/
```

Once you've copied the operating system into the jail dataset, mark that dataset as untrusted. That makes the dataset inaccessible to the host.

```
# zfs set mountpoint=/zroot mypool/jails/lucas/zroot
# zfs set jailed=on mypool/jails/lucas/zroot
```

With a ready dataset, make an entry for this jail in the jail config file */etc/jail.conf*. Here we define the jail **no.gelato.for.michaelwlucas.com**.[6]

---

6 Okay. Now Jude is just being mean. ==mwl

```
nogelatoforyou {
 host.hostname = "no.gelato.for.michaelwlucas.com";
 ip4.addr = "em0|198.51.100.200";
 path = "/mypool/jails/lucas";
 persist = true;
 mount.devfs = true;
 allow.mount = true;
 allow.mount.zfs = true;
 enforce_statfs = 1;
 exec.poststart = "/sbin/zfs jail nogelatoforyou mypool/
jails/lucas/zroot";
 exec.poststop = "/sbin/zfs unjail nogelatoforyou my-
pool/jails/lucas/zroot";
}
```

With the *jail.conf* entry in place, we can start the jail using the standard FreeBSD tools.

```
# service jail onestart nogelatoforyou
```

The last chunk of setup needs to happen within the jail. Alternatively, you could do something wild and crazy like plan ahead when installing the operating system, but that would take the fun out of things. Let's enter the jail and look at our datasets.

```
# jexec nogelatoforyou /bin/sh
jail# zfs list
NAME                         USED  AVAIL  REFER  MOUNTPOINT
mypool                      5.21G  13.1G    96K  none
mypool/jails                 180M  13.1G    96K  /mypool/jails
mypool/jails/lucas           180M  13.1G   180M  /mypool/jails/lucas
mypool/jails/lucas/zroot      96K  13.1G    96K  /zroots
```

This new jail doesn't have ZFS enabled in *rc.conf*, so the new dataset is not mounted by default. Enable ZFS and restart the jail.

```
jail# sysrc zfs_enable="YES"
```

Having made a configuration change, restart and reenter the jail.

```
# service jail onerestart nogelatoforyou
# jexec nogelatoforyou /bin/sh
```

You'll see the newly created datasets.

```
jail# zfs create mypool/jails/lucas/zroot/test
jail# zfs list
NAME                              USED  AVAIL  REFER  MOUNTPOINT
mypool                           5.21G  13.1G    96K  none
mypool/jails                      180M  13.1G    96K  /mypool/jails
mypool/jails/lucas                180M  13.1G   180M  /mypool/jails/lucas
mypool/jails/lucas/zroot          192K  13.1G    96K  /zroot
mypool/jails/lucas/zroot/test      96K  13.1G    96K  /zroot/test
```

The jail administrator must use the full path, including parts that are outside of the jail, to create new datasets.

Defining Limits and Safety Belts

But what if Lucas is incompetent, or evil? You gave him access to take his own snapshots, and he tries to create a million snapshots "just to see what would happen." You know people like that.

ZFS has your back when dealing with these difficult users. ZFS provides the `snapshot_limit` and `filesystem_limit` properties, which allow you to restrict the number of snapshots or child filesystems that can be created under a specific dataset. Set these properties to one greater than the number of snapshots or datasets you want the user to create. That is, if you set `snapshot_limit` to 10, the user can create nine snapshots. The tenth generates an error.

To contain the pure evil that is Lucas, limit the number of snapshots he can create to two.

```
# zfs set snapshot_limit=3 zroot/usr/home/lucas
# su lucas
$ zfs snapshot zroot/usr/home/lucas@three
$ zfs snapshot zroot/usr/home/lucas@four
cannot create snapshot 'zroot/usr/home/lucas': out of
space
```

The read-only `filesystem_count` and `snapshot_count` properties allow you to quickly see how many filesystems or snapshots exist, and compare that number to the limit.

Delegation and jails are powerful tools for administrative management of storage space. Now let's discuss sharing with ZFS.

Chapter 3: Sharing Datasets

OpenZFS integrates sharing of datasets over Server Message Block (SMB), Network File System (NFS), and Internet Small Computer System Interface (iSCSI). FreeBSD bundles support for only NFS and iSCSI, however. This chapter takes you through FreeBSD's iSCSI and NFS implementations and how they relate to ZFS, plus a few notes on using SMB with ZFS.

SMB

You can share ZFS datasets over SMB using a program like Samba (https://www.samba.org). It works exactly like Samba on any other filesystem. ZFS imposes literally zero restrictions or requirements on Samba, although you probably want to set `casesensitivity` to *mixed* on datasets shared with Windows clients via SMB.

ZFS datasets shared via Samba can seem weird to SMB clients, however. As a pool fills up, clients see the size of the dataset shrink. We discuss this in detail in *FreeBSD Mastery: ZFS*, but it's worth repeating here: if you monitor free space via SMB, you'll get terribly odd results. FreeNAS includes special support to show space utilization to Windows users correctly.

You can leverage Samba with ZFS to replicate many features found on Windows file servers. For example, with a bit of work, ZFS snapshots can be accessed through Windows Volume Shadow Copy. FreeNAS uses many such tricks to support Windows clients.

If your main role for ZFS is to support Windows clients with SMB, the authors strongly recommend using FreeNAS.

iSCSI

You can share zvols through any iSCSI target software you prefer. FreeBSD 10 and newer includes the Cam Target Layer daemon ctld(8), which serves as an iSCSI target. The ctld(8) software generally has higher performance than the istgt package used in older FreeBSD versions.

The ZFS administration tools do not integrate with either FreeBSD iSCSI target software yet, however. Manage sharing of zvols within `ctld`, not with zfs(8). We'll cover configuring a zvol-backed iSCSI target and some performance considerations for ZFS-backed iSCSI devices.

For much more detail on iSCSI and how not to use it, check out Lucas' *FreeBSD Mastery: Specialty Filesystems.*

Target Configuration

An iSCSI target provides SCSI-style storage services over the network. You might think of it as an iSCSI server, but a target is subtly different from a server. An iSCSI target never initiates any activity on its own. All requests must come from a client, or *initiator*.

Basic iSCSI services require a portal group, a target, and a Logical Unit Number or LUN. A portal group is a name given to a specific combination of IP address and TCP port. ("All IP addresses on this host" is a valid component of a portal group.) A target is a specific group of storage devices exported via iSCSI. One portal group can have any number of targets. A LUN is a single storage device within a target.

Here's a snippet of */etc/ctl.conf* that defines a single portal group.

```
portal-group group0 {
 discovery-auth-group no-authentication
 listen 0.0.0.0
 listen [::]
}
```

The portal group is named *group0.* While we can (and should) configure authentication for a production iSCSI target, we don't need authentication to get started. This portal group is available on all IPv4 and IPv6 IP addresses on the machine.

Next we define a target for this portal group. This target contains one LUN.

```
target iqn.2013-11.org.mwlucas:target0 {
 auth-group no-authentication
 portal-group group0
 lun 0 {
  path /dev/zvol/vm/db1
  size 1T
 }
}
```

Names for an iSCSI target are based on the domain name of the organization providing the target. Theoretically you can name your iSCSI targets almost any way you please, but some initiator software attempts to use the name to set optimizations. It's best to not copy target names from your commercial SAN provider.

The naming scheme for iSCSI devices always starts with the string *iqn*. You then have the year and month the domain name was registered, followed by the domain name in reverse. Here, mwlucas.org was registered in November of 2013, so the target name starts with *iqn.2013-11.org.mwlucas*. We then have a colon and the name of this specific target.

Like our portal group, this target does not require authentication. The *portal-group* keyword ties us to the group0 portal group created earlier.

This target has a single *LUN*, number 0. We give the path to the file or device node and the size of the target. Note the device node we use here, `/dev/zvol/vm/db1`. While a zvol might have multiple device nodes, always access the device node for iSCSI exported-zvols under `/dev/zvol`. It's best to create such zvols with a **volmode** of dev, so that the server's GEOM layer doesn't taste and preconfigure the zvol.

Once `/etc/ctl.conf` exists, start ctld(8).

```
# service ctld start
```

Status and error messages appear in `/var/log/messages`.

If ctld(8) doesn't fit your needs, use any target software you prefer. Use the zvol's device node to offer it to your initiator.

Network File System

Entire books have been written about the Network File System, or NFS. Many different operating systems support NFS, either as a server or a client or both. For this book, we'll focus on offering NFS shares through the ZFS-integrated tools.

NFS Configuration Types

You can manage ZFS-backed NFS exports with the traditional FreeBSD `/etc/exports` file, and nothing horrific will happen to you. If you're an old FreeBSD hand, `/etc/exports` might even feel more comfortable. But zfs(8) handles many aspects of NFS management for you, and works identically across all ZFS platforms.

However you manage NFS on your host, we strongly encourage you to choose a single method and stick with it. Don't use both `/etc/exports` and ZFS to manage your NFS shares. FreeBSD reads share information from both locations, making troubleshooting even more annoying.

A FreeBSD host must have an */etc/exports* file to serve NFS shares, even if you manage NFS entirely within ZFS. The simplest way to get this is `touch /etc/exports`, although you might want an exports file that contains only comments directing other sysadmins to zfs(8).

As with iSCSI, we're not going to completely cover NFS. We'll cover managing NFS from a ZFS perspective, drawing comparisons to traditional NFS configuration where useful.

Enabling NFSv2/v3

Enabling NFS at the ZFS level does nothing if the host isn't running the services required for NFS. Set the following in */etc/rc.conf* to start the processes needed to serve NFS at boot.

```
nfs_server_enable=YES
rpcbind_enable=YES
mountd_enable=YES
rpc_lockd_enable=YES
rpc_statd_enable=YES
```

Not all environments require all of these services, but turning them on doesn't use many system resources and offers the widest range of compatibility and decent performance.

You also must allow hosts on your network to access rpcbind(8), with an */etc/hosts.allow* entry. Here I let the network 203.0.113.0/24 access my NFS services.

```
rpcbind: 203.0.113.0/255.255.255.0 : allow
```

Without this *hosts.allow* entry, your clients will drive you to the brink of madness with meaningless NFS errors.

Configuring NFSv2/v3 via ZFS

ZFS configures NFS on a per-dataset basis. The ZFS property **sharenfs** dictates how a dataset is shared. This property can be set to *on*, *off*, or to NFS share options for the dataset.

If set to *off*, ZFS does not configure sharing for this dataset. The dataset could still be shared via */etc/exports*, however.

Setting this property to on shares the dataset via NFS. It's equivalent to listing the filesystem by itself in */etc/exports*. Setting **sharenfs** to *on* for *zroot/home* would be like the following */etc/exports* entry.

```
/home
```

Any host anywhere in the world could access and NFS mount this host.

It would be far more sensible to set access for only those hosts we want to allow.

```
# zfs set sharenfs="203.0.113.208" zroot/home
```

This generates an */etc/zfs/exports* like this.

```
/home    203.0.113.208
```

If you must enter more complicated values in the properties, enclose them in quotes or otherwise escape them.

```
# zfs set sharenfs="-network 203.0.113.0 -mask
255.255.255.0" zroot/home
```

Any entries that make valid */etc/exports* entries are usable as values for **sharenfs**.

The **sharenfs** property cannot support any NFS configuration that requires multiple lines in */etc/exports*. For these environments, you must use a traditional *exports* file.

Enabling NFSv4

NFSv4 is a whole different protocol from NFSv2 or v3. Don't enable NFSv4 unless you understand it. This section gets those people who already have some NFSv4 know-how up and running.

To enable NFSv4, set the following in */etc/rc.conf*.

```
nfs_server_enable=YES
mountd_enable=YES
nfsv4_server_enable=YES
nfsuserd_enable=YES
```

You'll also need a single line in */etc/exports*, defining the root of your NFS tree. This is normally the filesystem root.

```
V4: /
```

Enable and disable NFS sharing with the **sharenfs** property on individual datasets.

Configuring NFSv4 via ZFS

As with older NFS versions, use the **sharenfs** property to configure exports for a single dataset. NFSv4 exports everything in a directory tree, however, so inheritance plays a pretty big role.

Setting **sharenfs** to *on* tells NFS to share the dataset with everyone, without restrictions. You rely entirely on firewalls or packet filters to prevent unauthorized access to this dataset and its descendent datasets. Like other ZFS properties, **sharenfs** is inherited. If you share *zroot/home*, you're sharing all the home directories beneath it.

Setting **sharenfs** to *off* tells NFS to not share this dataset. Use this to deliberately override a parent dataset's **sharenfs** setting.

Setting this to an IP address, or a mask statement, shares the dataset exactly as it does for NFSv2/3 exports.

Debugging ZFS NFS

FreeBSD assembles the **sharenfs** properties into an exports file, */etc/zfs/exports*. If you're familiar with NFS, checking this file might give you insight into why the file shares are working as they do.

Check */var/log/messages* on the client and server for hints as to why a mount fails. The most common errors we see, after *hosts.allow* and firewall problems, are invalid **sharenfs** properties. After decades of practice, Lucas *still* specifies allowed networks as CIDR blocks rather than in the NFS-friendly format.

Chapter 4: Replication

What exactly is [/ˌrepləˈkāSH(ə)n/] anyway? In ZFS, it means making an exact copy of your filesystem someplace else. That other place can be another dataset in your pool, a second pool on your system, an external drive, a remote system, a tape, or just a file. You can declare "I want *this* filesystem in *that* place," and make it happen. ZFS replication has a few design features that make it especially powerful.

Programs like dump(8) and rsync(1) expect the receiver to somehow acknowledge receipt of the data. The ZFS replication process is unidirectional—the sender does not need any feedback from the receiving side. As replication doesn't expect any acknowledgement, the ZFS recipient doesn't need any intelligence; it only needs to accept a stream of bytes and do something with them.

The replication system is integrated with snapshots. A snapshot is a static, unchanging entity, which means that the transmitted ZFS dataset is fully coherent, unlike dumping or rsyncing a live filesystem. Snapshot-based replication also means you can do incremental replication, sending only the blocks that have changed between two snapshots. With incremental replication, you never have to send the same data twice.

ZFS's replication feature is designed to fully utilize all of your disks. The only limitation to how fast you can replicate data between machines is the speed of your network link.

ZFS replication consists of two parts: `zfs send`, which serializes a snapshot or series of snapshots into a single data stream, and `zfs receive`, which turns that stream back into a ZFS filesystem.

But I Have Rsync!

For decades now, rsync(1) has been the standard tool for synchronizing files between machines. To synchronize files, `rsync` walks the directory tree, evaluates the timestamps and cryptographic checksums of each file, and compares them to the files on the remote side. Many organizations have deployed extensive `rsync`-based infrastructure.

ZFS is designed from the disk up for maximum performance. It beats `rsync` so badly that `rsync`'s mom needs urgent medical attention. ZFS maintains a list of blocks on disk that differ between each snapshot. The replication process doesn't need to determine which files have changed—the filesystem itself already has that information. The replication process starts sending those blocks, as quickly as possible, immediately. As the changed blocks contain all the metadata to reassemble the files, the replication process doesn't even need to know which files those blocks belong to.

While `rsync` is walking your filesystem, looking at each file, checking its timestamp, calculating a checksum, and comparing those to the versions on the other side, ZFS has already finished. If you have 10 TB of data, and only 1 GB has changed, `rsync` still needs to check every file. ZFS just grabs the 1 GB of changed blocks and sends them.

A sysadmin who needs faster `rsync` synchronization can tell `rsync` to cheat and assume that if the last modified time on both the local and remote files are the same, the file has not changed. (This is not actually always true, but don't hold that against `rsync`—the sysadmin should know better.) When a file's timestamp has changed, `rsync` calculates checksums on chunks of the file on both sides, and compares the checksums. If it finds a difference, it then calculates a delta and sends that across. This means that if you make a small change to a large file, `rsync` must read and checksum the entire file on both the local and remote side. Using `rsync` to maintain a copy of that 500 GB

VM disk image on a backup machine eats a whole bunch of disk bandwidth and processor time.

Each block in ZFS has a *birthtime*, the transaction group ID of when the block was created. The replication process sends any block newer than the last time replication was run. It doesn't matter if the blocks come from a new file, or the middle of a huge file.

The advantages of snapshot-based replication really come into play when you regularly synchronize filesystems. Suppose you replicate a snapshot on a remote backup server. An hour later, you create a new snapshot and incrementally send that snapshot to the backup server. ZFS finishes in a few seconds, while `rsync` is still walking the first level of directories.

Rsync(1) supports a *snapshot* backup mode. Snapshots in `rsync` are completely different than ZFS snapshots, however. With `rsync` snapshots, if you modify 1 byte of a 1 GB file, `rsync` keeps two entire copies of the file. ZFS, on the other hand, keeps the two different copies of a single block. The two versions of the file share the rest of the blocks.

In `rsync`'s defense, it is a cross-platform, cross-filesystem tool. You can use `rsync` to synchronize directory trees between operating systems and between filesystems. Lucas has used `rsync` to synchronize directory trees between wildly different Unix-like platforms, like FreeBSD and AIX and Linux.

But if you're using ZFS, replication is uniquely suited to deal with ZFS. Replication understands and duplicates ZFS properties. It can maintain the relationship between a clone and its parent, whereas `rsync` would lose this link and surrender all of your space savings. Rsync(1) doesn't work so well on raw block devices, but ZFS replication works with zvols. Replication uses the filesystem's integrated checksums as well, so there's no risk of the files you receive somehow differing from the originals.

ZFS replication is also version agnostic. New pool features are enabled only if you deliberately add the command-line flags to request them. This lets ZFS replication easily move data between pools of different versions.

Why Replicate?

Replication comes into play many ways: most obviously in backups, but also in testing, virtualization, and data migrations.

You do remember that RAID is not a backup, right? Even RAID-Z3 is not a proper backup. When your machine catches on fire, when law enforcement confiscates all hardware at your hosting provider, or when you accidently delete that vital dataset, RAID-Z3 will not save you. Replicate your important pools to an external drive, a backup machine, or a tape library. Now you can get it back even after complete loss of the hardware. The beauty of ZFS is that after the initial replication, *every* backup can be an incremental.

Let's take it a step further. Maybe just being able to recover your data is inadequate. You must guarantee that your data is always accessible, 24x7x365. You need High Availability. Replicate your data to a second and third server, with incremental snapshots every few minutes. Now you always have your data ready to go on n+2 hot spare servers. Put one of those backup servers at a remote location, and you are protected even against total facility destruction.[7]

So, that nice dataset of customer data you have there. You'd like to test the new version of your billing system with that. Rather than cloning the data on the same machine, you need a completely separate

---

7 Arranging geographic high availability on your IT staff is a separate problem. We recommend letting everyone work from home. For best results, buy them homes in places like Fiji and the Seychelles. Stick the unpopular guy in Moose Burp, Alaska.

copy in the dev environment. Whether the target is a remote machine or a new dataset on the same pool, ZFS replication is the fastest and most reliable way to copy data.

Do you have dozens or hundreds of identical machines, VMs, or containers? Use ZFS replication to deploy your perfectly crafted image everywhere. If you design your systems properly, you can even use incremental replication to deploy updates.

Replication also greatly simplifies migrating data, even huge amounts of data over ridiculous distances. Maybe you have to migrate a massive dataset to the other side of the country, or across the planet. With enough data, even 10 Gb/s Ethernet in the same datacenter seems too slow! Suppose you have many terabytes of data that are always in use and undergoing constant minor churn, such as a customer database. Copying that data over the Internet to the opposite end of the country, or the world, will take days—but by then, the data will have changed. An `rsync`-based replication process takes so long that it will probably never catch up. Your database administrators are smart folks, and probably can come up with a clever plan for moving the data with some sort of complicated data segmentation. These plans can be done successfully, but increase risk and always impose a heavy workload and frustration.

If the bandwidth available for synchronization exceeds the rate of change in the data, use ZFS instead. Your first ZFS replication, which includes every scrap of data from this huge dataset, might take a few days or weeks. You might even find it more practical to perform the first synchronization via tape and overnight shipping. When this synchronization finishes, though, a second replication from a new snapshot won't take nearly as long. With a few iterations, so long as your rate of change is slower than the bandwidth available for backup, ZFS replication catches up to nearly real time.

On Big Switch Day, freeze the dataset for a few moments while you replicate the most recent set of changes. You'll probably have a few moments of panic over load balancers, firewalls, new servers, and all the other gadgets needed to support such a massive dataset, but the data itself won't be the problem.

Basic Replication

ZFS doesn't replicate datasets. It replicates snapshots. Snapshots don't change during replication (or any other time), so they're guaranteed to be internally consistent. Start by creating a snapshot of your data.

```
# zfs snapshot mypool/somedata@snappycomeback
```

Now let's replicate this snapshot both locally and on a remote host.

Local Replication

ZFS replication is unidirectional, meaning that it doesn't need any feedback from the receiver. This means you can dump the snapshot into any other program, using standard Unix shell redirections and pipes. Here, I feed the output of `zfs send` into a regular file. (If you add the `-v` flag, `zfs send` prints a progress summary every second.)

```
# zfs send mypool/somedata@snappycomeback > backup_file
```

This file is our first use of ZFS replication, so it's not incremental. It contains everything in the snapshot. It's about the same size as the dataset. It's not exactly useful as-is, however—very few people can read a streamed filesystem without turning it back into a filesystem.[8] So let's feed this dataset back into ZFS with `zfs receive`.

```
# zfs receive mypool/copy < backup_file
```

---

8 The people who can read a streamed filesystem without turning it back into a filesystem have far better uses for their time.

Zfs(8) reads the replication stream from the *backup_file* and create a new dataset from it, an exact duplicate of the original dataset.

You don't need a file in the middle of local replication. This is a Unix-like system. We have the miracle of pipes. This host has home directories on the root pool, but I'm moving a copy to a new pool.

```
# zfs send zroot/home@weds | zfs receive mypool/home
```

I can now shuffle a couple dataset mount points and move my home directories to the new pool.

ZFS' unidirectional nature lets you replicate to anything you can aim a command at, such as a tape. With pipes you can pour `zfs send` through SSH and into `zfs receive`, letting you replicate a dataset on a remote machine.

Viewing Replicas

Want to see the inside of a stream file? The zstreamdump(8) utility examines streams and exposes their details. You can examine a file, or read directly from `zfs send`.

```
# zstreamdump < backup_file
```

The `zstreamdump` program responds with one section like this for each and every snapshot within the `zfs send` stream.

```
BEGIN record
 hdrtype = 1
 features = 4
 magic = 2f5bacbac
 creation_time = 56a53713
 type = 2
 flags = 0x0
 toguid = 424654598740125b
 fromguid = 0
 toname = mypool/somedata@snappycomeback
END checksum = 14035a747cefd2/65f5a463eb5427f0/
3e70de6ff7d7456/497949c053fadcb3
```

This output has a bunch of information about the `zfs send` stream. The hard part is, none of it is presented in a human-friendly manner. Even so, we can extract a few chunks of information from it.

The *creation_time* field gives the time `zfs send` was run, in the convenient measure of seconds from the Unix epoch—in hex, of course, because why wouldn't you use hex for dates? Convert this value (56a53713) to a human readable value with date(1). Put a *0x* in front of the value to identify it as a hex value.

```
$ date -r 0x56a53713
Sun Jan 24 15:41:55 EST 2016
```

On non-FreeBSD hosts, `date` might not accept hex values. While there are many ways to do this conversion, you might try something like this.

```
$ printf "%d\n" 0x56a53713 | xargs date -r
```

Each snapshot has a human-readable name, given in the *toname*. This snapshot is called *mypool/somedata@snappycomeback*, and illuminates the importance of using meaningful names for datasets and snapshots.

Each snapshot within a stream also has a globally unique identifier, or GUID. This snapshot's GUID appears in the *toguid* field.

The *fromgid* field is used for incremental ZFS sends (see "Incremental Replication" later in this chapter), including only the changes between two snapshots. It's zero in this example, meaning that this `zfs send` stream contains a complete snapshot. It's not an incremental. As it's a complete snapshot, restoring this `zfs send` stream to a live dataset would make sense. (You could restore an incremental ZFS stream, but you'd need a copy of the snapshot it's based on.)

If a stream has multiple snapshots in it—say, from an incremental or recursive `zfs send`—you can use the *toguid* and *fromguid* values to piece together how the snapshots fit together. It's probably easier to restore the `zfs send` stream to a dataset and look at it that way, however.

Each section ends with a *checksum*. You can't use the checksum to manually verify the snapshot in this section, but it's nice to know that ZFS uses checksums.

After the details on each snapshot, `zstreamdump` prints a summary.

```
SUMMARY:
 Total DRR_BEGIN records = 5
 Total DRR_END records = 6
...
 Total records = 170
 Total write size = 10523136 (0xa09200)
 Total stream length = 10554216 (0xa10b68)
```

The summary includes a whole bunch of ZFS internal metadata. The most interesting parts here are the number of DRR_BEGIN records, which corresponds to the number of snapshots in this stream. The sizes at the end are in bytes. The write size is the size of the data included in the stream, while the stream length is the size of the stream itself. (A ZFS `send` stream has metadata for restoring data to disk that doesn't need to get written to the disk.)

Remote Replication

In order to replicate ZFS to a remote host, the remote host needs a user that can accept the replication and a secure pipe to that remote host. The most common type of secure replication pipe is SSH, so we'll assume that's your tool. In the long term, the easiest way to use SSH is with key-based authentication. If you're not familiar with key-based authentication, consult any number of online tutorials or Lucas' *SSH Mastery* (Tilted Windmill Press, 2012).

You could use the **`root`** account to receive replication streams, but that means permitting SSH logins as **`root`**. SSH as **`root`** is a bad idea. Don't do it. And do you really want some shell script maintained by this random guy somewhere on the Internet stomping around with **root** on all of your machines? Instead, create an unprivileged user and assign it replication rights, as discussed in Chapter 2.

Similarly, while you can send ZFS datasets as **root**, you might want an operator or normal user to have the ability to send datasets.

Replication Users and Datasets

On both the sending and receiving hosts, we create a user dedicated to replication. Our sample user is called **replicator**. It needs a shell, but no special group memberships.

```
local# pw user add replicator -m -s /bin/sh
remote# pw user add replicator -m -s /bin/sh
```

On the sending host, the replication user needs the **send** and **snapshot** privileges on the dataset to be sent. Here we give **replicator** these privileges on user home directories.

```
# zfs allow -u replicator send,snapshot zroot/usr/home
```

The sending user needs an SSH keypair. A user who is using his own account on both the sending and receiving sides can use their own SSH keys for this. For dedicated accounts, generate a keypair with ssh-keygen(1).

```
# su replicator
$ ssh-keygen
```

The `ssh-keygen` program prompts you for a passphrase. If a human being will use this account to send ZFS datasets, use a passphrase. If this is for an automated process, use an empty passphrase.

The key is the file *.ssh/id_rsa.pub* in the user's home account. We also recommend restricting which hosts can use this key to log in to the remote machine, to help protect the remote host and your backups in the event this key is stolen.

Now have this unprivileged user install the public key in their account on the remote machine. Here we send the new key to an account with the same username on the host **hotspare**.

```
$ ssh-copy-id -i .ssh/id_rsa.pub hotspare
```

Verify that you can log into the receiving host as this user.

On the receiving host, the user must own the mount point of the recipient dataset. The system must also permit unprivileged users to mount filesystems on directories they own, using the vfs.usermount sysctl.

```
# zfs create -o mountpoint=/backup remotepool/backup
# chown replicator:replicator /backup
# sysctl vfs.usermount=1
```

Our unprivileged user needs the **compression**, **create**, **mount**, **mountpoint**, and **receive** ZFS privileges on the target dataset. Here I assign the replicator user privileges on the *remotepool/backup* dataset. If you intend to automate ZFS replication, including destruction of outdated snapshots, you'll want to add the **destroy** property.

```
# zfs allow -u replicator compression,mountpoint,create,
mount,receive remotepool/backup
```

This unprivileged user can now replicate this dataset.

If you want to replicate all of the dataset's properties, you must allow the replicator user to set all of those properties. See Chapter 2 for details on how to create a permissions set.

Dataset Full Remote Replication

To replicate a ZFS dataset, first create a snapshot. I gave my unprivileged user permission to create snapshots exactly for this purpose, so let him do it.

```
$ zfs snapshot zroot/usr/home@monday
```

Now use `zfs send` to transmit this snapshot, pipe that into SSH, and dump it into `zfs receive`. Remember, ssh(1) lets you execute commands on the remote host. Since this is the first time we have replicated this dataset, the send stream includes every block in the snapshot.

```
$ zfs send zroot/usr/home@monday | \
    ssh user@host zfs receive remotepool/backup
```

In addition to replicating to a pool on another machine, you can replicate to the same pool or a second pool on the same machine, to a file, or to a pipe. Replicating to a file or pipe can be useful for backups, such as to tape, or to a different filesystem.

You can have a host log into another host to trigger the `zfs send` if you prefer, changing ZFS replication from a push model to a pull one.

```
$ ssh user@host zfs send zroot/usr/home@monday | \
    zfs receive remotepool/backup
```

This book assumes that you're sending from a local dataset for consistency, but everything works in the other direction.

Incremental Replication

The real power comes from incremental replication. Now that we have replicated all of the data from the dataset as of Monday, Tuesday's replication needs to send only the blocks that have changed. The `receive` side of the command doesn't change at all, but on the `send` side we use the `-i` flag to indicate the most recent snapshot sent.

```
$ zfs snapshot zroot/usr/home@tuesday
$ zfs send -i @monday zroot/usr/home@tuesday | \
    ssh user@host zfs receive remotepool/backup/home
```

ZFS sends only the blocks that have changed between the @monday and @tuesday snapshots, saving time and bandwidth.

Now look at the dataset on the receiving system.

```
# zfs list -t snap -r zroot/backup
NAME                              USED  AVAIL  REFER  MOUNTPOINT
zroot/backup/usrhome@monday        8K      -  49.0M  -
zroot/backup/usrhome@tuesday        0      -  49.0M  -
```

Two snapshots now show up.

One common mistake with incremental backups is not specifying the last snapshot that exists on the remote system. If you don't specify the most recent snapshot that was transmitted, you'll get an error.

```
# zfs send zroot/usr/home@tuesday | \
      ssh hotspare zfs recv remotepool/backup/usrhome
cannot receive new filesystem stream: destination
remotepool/backup/usrhome' exists
must specify -F to overwrite it
```

The danger of an error message like this is that it offers ways to make the error disappear, rather than suggesting ways to fix the underlying problem. Overwriting the remote dataset wipes out your older snapshots and resends all the data.

When using `-i`, you can skip the @ sign in front of the snapshot name. The `-i` flag means "this is a snapshot," so it can safely assume that you meant to put the @ in front but just couldn't be bothered.

Incremental Replication Assumptions

Incremental backups to tape are pretty much fixed: you might overwrite them, but in the 21st century you wouldn't go in and edit a file directly on the tape. Incremental backups written to disk are very easy to change, though.

Incremental replication requires that the receiver's copy of the dataset doesn't change between replication runs. Changes in the copy ruin the whole process. If you edit the backup copy of the dataset, the next incremental update will no longer plug into the backup copy.
If you want to edit a dataset replica on the backup machine, create a clone of the received dataset and edit that.

If someone accidentally or ignorantly edited the replica, roll the changes back to the last common snapshot. Have the receiver force a rollback to the matching remote snapshot by adding the `-F` flag to the `zfs receive` command.

```
# zfs send -i @monday zroot/usr/home@tuesday | ssh \
    user@hotspare zfs receive -F remotepool/backup/home
```

Prevent alterations to replica datasets by setting the ZFS property **`readonly`** to *on* for the replicated datasets. With the privileges given earlier, users can add snapshots to write-only datasets.

```
# zfs set readonly=on remotepool/backup
```

You can still add snapshots under *remotepool/backup*. You can examine the files in the dataset. But nobody can edit the files without changing the ZFS **`readonly`** property. And anyone with that access should either know better or have a desperately urgent need to make that dataset live, right now.

Differential Replication

ZFS replication can be done on any two snapshots on the same dataset, so you can also do differential backups. Using the `-I` flag (uppercase i), instead of `-i` sends all snapshots that exist between the two snapshots.

Suppose Tuesday's snapshot replication fails because of a random network issue.[9] On Wednesday, you want to send both Tuesday's and Wednesday's snapshots.

```
# zfs send -I @monday zroot/usr/home@wednesday | \
    ssh hotspare zfs recv remotepool/backup/usrhome
```

The recipient now has Tuesday's snapshot, even though you never explicitly sent it.

9 Sysadmins may blame any problem that occurs once on "random network issues." It's in the Code of Conduct.

Folks with experience running backups will realize that we're using the words "incremental" and "differential" in a slightly different way than most backup software does. Backup software is written for sending blocks to tape, and minimizing the number of tapes you need to use to restore files. We could invent a new language, we could go digging for precisely suitable but unfamiliar words,[10] or we can stretch existing language just a little.

SSH Bandwidth Limitations

You might find that an SSH connection is not fast enough for your needs. Those of you who need replication faster than a couple hundred megabytes per second probably should consider an external security solution, such as a dedicated VPN. SSH won't carry data that quickly without very specific modifications, so consider mbuffer(1).

The Complexities of Incremental Replication

ZFS replication is unidirectional, from the sender to the receiver. The sender gets no feedback from the receiver, permitting dumping the stream to just about anything. This becomes important when deciding between incremental and differential replication.

Incremental backups (with `-i`) send all blocks that have changed between the birthtimes of the first snapshot and the last snapshot, without sending any snapshots that exist in between. If a dataset has a snapshot for each day of the week, `zfs send -i monday zroot/usr/home@thursday` generates a stream that depends on the @monday snapshot existing on the receiving side, and results in the @thursday snapshot being created there. Any intervening snapshots do not get replicated.

---

10 Lucas would find deep joy in making you learn some obscure word that fits ZFS backups perfectly. Probably from a tonal language, but adding both Bantu and Khoisan clicks. Jude thinks that Lucas has no manners.

Differential backups (with `-I`) work exactly like incremental backups, but they create any intermediary snapshots. A command like `zfs send -I @monday zroot/usr/home@thursday` requires that the @monday snapshot exist on the remote side, and it creates the absent @tuesday and @wednesday snapshots in passing.

Assume you've automatically taken daily snapshots of a dataset, and you want to ship them over to the remote server. Replicate the @monday snapshot to the remote pool:

```
# zfs send zroot/usr/home@monday | \
      zfs receive hotspare remotepool/backup/usrhome
```

Check on your remote host to verify the presence of the @monday snapshot.

```
# zfs list -t all -r remotepool/backup/usrhome
NAME                               USED  AVAIL  REFER  MOUNTPOINT
remotepool/backup/usrhome         19.5K   472M  19.5K  /remotepool/weekday
remotepool/backup/usrhome@monday  0         -   19.5K  -
```

Now incrementally replicate the @tuesday snapshot.

```
# zfs send -i monday remotepool/backup/usrhome@tuesday \
      | zfs receive remotepool/weekday
```

Checking the remote host, you'll find both snapshots.

```
# zfs list -t all -r remotepool/backup/usrhome
NAME                                USED  AVAIL  REFER  MOUNTPOINT
remotepool/backup/usrhome            29K   472M  19.5K  /remotepool/weekday
remotepool/backup/usrhome@monday   9.50K      -  19.5K  -
remotepool/backup/usrhome@tuesday      0      -  19.5K  -
```

On Wednesday you were off gallivanting about—uh, I mean, "out sick"—so you didn't do the replication. Thursday, you want to catch up, so you do a differential replication of the @thursday snapshot.

```
# zfs send -I tuesday zroot/usr/home@thursday | \
      zfs receive remotepool/backup/usrhome
```

Our hot spare host now has four snapshots.

```
# zfs list -t all -r remotepool/backup/usrhome
NAME                                    USED  AVAIL  REFER  MOUNTPOINT
remotepool/backup/usrhome                48K   472M  19.5K  /remotepool/weekday
remotepool/backup/usrhome@monday       9.50K      -  19.5K  -
remotepool/backup/usrhome@tuesday      9.50K      -  19.5K  -
remotepool/backup/usrhome@wednesday    9.50K      -  19.5K  -
remotepool/backup/usrhome@thursday         0      -  19.5K  -
```

But suppose koala-related mayhem costs you sleep Thursday night. You stagger in Friday morning determined to get through the day without breaking anything. Setting up the day's replication, you accidentally try to do an incremental (`-i`) `zfs send` from @monday to @friday.

```
# zfs send -i monday mypool/weekday@friday | \
      zfs receive remotepool/weekday
cannot receive incremental stream: destination
remotepool/weekday has been modified since most recent
snapshot.
```

You might know darn well you haven't modified those snapshots. Nobody's allowed to log onto that machine. But it has been modified—the @tuesday, @wednesday, and @thursday snapshots are in the way.

If you are not sure what snapshots might exist on the remote end, you can use `-I` to send all intermediary snapshots. Alternatively, you could specify `-F` in the `zfs receive` command to force it to remove anything that is in the way.

```
# zfs send -i @monday zroot/usr/home@friday | \
      zfs receive -F remotepool/backup/usrhome
```

The unpleasant side effect of using `zfs receive -F` to "remove anything that is in the way" is that it destroys the intermediate snapshots.

```
# zfs list -t all -r remotepool/weekday
NAME                                USED  AVAIL  REFER  MOUNTPOINT
remotepool/backup/usrhome            29K   472M  19.5K  /remotepool/weekday
remotepool/backup/usrhome@monday  9.50K      -   19.5K  -
remotepool/backup/usrhome@friday      0      -   19.5K  -
```

We want those snapshots back, so let's try that again. On your hot spare host, eliminate the newest snapshot.

```
# zfs destroy remotepool/backup/usrhome@friday
```

Now have the sender retransmit all those snapshots, either one at a time or en masse. Here we send one snapshot, just to be sure that we didn't break anything else on this bleary-eyed Friday.

```
# zfs send -i monday mypool/weekday@tuesday | \
      zfs receive -F remotepool/weekday
```

The fact that the replication is unidirectional means that in differential backups you could send overlaps, transmitting a snapshot that already exists on the remote side. If we send all snapshots between @monday and @friday, while the @tuesday snapshot already exists on the remote pool, the source sends all of the changed data, even the blocks that the remote side already has. The remote side fast forwards through the blocks it has, and then creates the snapshots that it doesn't—in this case, @wednesday through @friday.

Best practice here is to avoid koalas. And their mayhem.

Recursive Replication

ZFS also supports *recursive replication*, which replicates a dataset and all of its children in one command. Here's a sample pool with three datasets.

```
NAME            USED  AVAIL  REFER  MOUNTPOINT
mypool          401M  3.09T   192K  /mypool
mypool/family  50.2M  3.09T  50.2M  /mypool/family
mypool/home     150M  3.09T   150M  /mypool/home
mypool/work     200M  3.09T   200M  /mypool/work
```

Take a recursive snapshot of the dataset and its children.

```
# zfs snapshot -r mypool@first
# zfs list -t all -r mypool
NAME                  USED  AVAIL  REFER  MOUNTPOINT
mypool                401M  3.09T   192K  /mypool
mypool@first             0      -   192K  -
mypool/family        50.2M  3.09T  50.2M  /mypool/family
mypool/family@first      0      -  50.2M  -
mypool/home           150M  3.09T   150M  /mypool/home
mypool/home@first        0      -   150M  -
mypool/work           200M  3.09T   200M  /mypool/work
mypool/work@first        0      -   200M  -
```

Now replicate that snapshot and all its children simultaneously, using a recursive send.

```
# zfs send -Rv mypool@first | \
      zfs receive remotepool/backup
send from @ to mypool@first estimated size is 9.50K
send from @ to mypool/work@first estimated size is 200M
send from @ to mypool/family@first estimated size is 50.1M
send from @ to mypool/home@first estimated size is 150M
total estimated size is 401M
...
```

Recursive send also works with incremental (`-i`) and differential (`-I`) backups, in exactly the same way. Now you can forcibly destroy a dataset and its children simultaneously!

Advanced Sending Options

A sender can alter how it sends datasets in several ways.

Sending Properties

To send dataset properties as well as the actual data, add the `-p` flag. When the properties of the received dataset differ from those already on the dataset, `zfs receive` attempts to change the properties to match those sent. That is, if you're replicating properties from a dataset that uses lz4 compression to a dataset that already uses lz4, `zfs receive` does nothing with that property. If the sender uses gzip-9 compression, though, the receiver changes to match the original.

The user receiving the dataset must have the permissions to set the properties you want replicated. If the user has permissions to replicate some but not all of the properties, the permissible properties get set and the disallowed properties are rejected.

Suppose our source dataset has `dedup` set to *on* and `compression` set to `gzip-9`. The receiving dataset has `dedup` set to *off* and `compression` set to `lz4`. We want the receiving dataset to use the same `compression`, but not the `dedup` setting. We permit our replication user to change `compression`.

```
# zfs allow -u replicator compress zroot/backup
```

When we send the dataset, we'll get an error.

```
cannot receive compression dedup on remotepool/backup:
permission denied
```

That's fine—we don't want the `dedup` property set on the replica. The `compression` property is replicated as desired, though.

Why would we replicate properties, rather than just set them on the destination? Manual configuration might be fine for simple properties like compression and `dedup`, but not so suitable for complicated properties like `sharenfs` or any of the quotas.

Deduplicated Data Stream

Is your data deduplicated? Is it suitable for deduplication? ZFS lets you deduplicate the `zfs send` data stream. With `-D`, each unique block is sent only once. It doesn't change what the recipient writes to disk, but only affects the data stream.

Deduplicated data streams use a different set of deduplication memory than that used by on-disk deduplication. If your data can be effectively deduplicated, but that deduplication uses many gigabytes of RAM, both the sending and receiving hosts need a similar amount of memory to deduplicate the data stream. Don't lightly deduplicate in `zfs send`!

Debugging and Testing

A `zfs send` supports a couple of options that can help with debugging, testing, and monitoring.

The `-v` option makes `zfs send` verbose. It prints information about the data to be sent and adds regular status updates.

The `-P` flag prints information about the send stream right when the stream starts flowing. The manual describes this information as "machine-readable." The information is readable by humans, but it's not nicely tabulated. It's perfect for feeding to your scripts, however.

The `-n` flag prevents `zfs send` from actually sending any data. Instead, when combined with either `-v` or `-P`, it gives statistics on what `zfs send` would do if it actually ran.

Large and Small Blocks

Newer versions of ZFS can support disk blocks larger than 128 KB, with the `large_blocks` zpool(8) feature. The `-L` flag lets `zfs send` include large blocks rather than breaking them up into small blocks. The recipient pool must also support large blocks.

For hosts with really small blocks, `-e` shrinks the size of the data stream by using the `embedded_data` feature. The destination pool must also support the `embedded_data` feature flag.

Advanced Receiving Options

The receiver can adjust how it stores the incoming ZFS stream, through arguments to `zfs receive`.

Path and Mount Management

A received ZFS stream includes the pool and dataset path of the origin. You can either retain this path or strip it out.

By adding the `-d` flag, you tell `zfs receive` to use the source's full path (except for the pool name) as the path to the destination dataset, rather than requiring the sysadmin to specify the destination dataset. Earlier, we replicated *zroot/usr/home* to *remotepool/backup/usrhome*. By using `-d` here, we tell `zfs receive` to use the source path on the destination.

```
$ zfs send zroot/usr/home@monday | \
      ssh hotspare zfs receive -d remotepool/backup
```

The receiver creates *remotepool/backup/usr/home* and sticks the @monday snapshot there. This function is very useful when replicating many layers of datasets.

Alternatively, you can strip out most of the path information. By adding the `-e` flag, you instruct `zfs receive` to use the last part of the path to name this dataset. Here we run the same backup, but strip out most of the path.

```
$ zfs send zroot/usr/home@monday | \
      ssh zfs2 zfs receive -e remotepool/backup
```

The `zfs receive` command looks at the path *zroot/usr/home* and discards everything but the last chunk, or *home*. The received data stream goes into *remotepool/backup/home*.

Finally, the `-u` option tells `zfs receive` not to mount received snapshots. The data's there for mounting if the sysadmin desires, but mounting the dataset might lead to changing the data.

Roll Back Changes

If someone has altered a received dataset, attempts to incrementally add a new snapshot to that replica will fail. Datasets of received snapshots must be pristine for `zfs receive` to accept incremental or differential updates.

The `-F` flag tells `zfs receive` to roll back any changes that prevent accepting this snapshot.

Debugging and Testing

Much like `zfs send`, `zfs receive` supports verbosity and no-effect options.

The `-v` option makes `zfs receive` verbose. It prints information about the data received and adds regular status updates.

The `-n` flag prevents `zfs receive` from actually writing any data to disk. Instead, when combined with `-v` it offers statistics on what `zfs receive` would do if actually used.

While verbosity can be useful, the `-n` option has limited utility in receiving data. The host will have sent data across the network to this host, and the recipient will have done some numerical analysis and discarded the data. To write the data to disk, you must re-send it.

Cloning on Receipt

You might need to send a dataset that you know you're going to want to muck with. As of FreeBSD 10.3, you can tell `zfs receive` to store an incoming incremental replication stream as a clone rather than as a snapshot. Cloning on receipt works only with incremental replication.

To have `zfs receive` create a clone, add the `-o` flag and define the origin as the dataset you want to clone. The `zfs receive` command takes that dataset, adds the incoming snapshot to it, and forks the clone off the original.

Throughout this chapter we've been backing up *zroot/usr/home* to a remote server. Assume we want a read-write clone of the Wednesday snapshot. We'll start by cloning the Tuesday snapshot.

```
$ zfs send -i @tuesday zroot/usr/home@wednesday | \
     ssh hotspare zfs receive \
     -o origin=remotepool/usr/home@tuesday \
     remotepool/usr/wedshome
```

The `-o origin` statement tells `zfs receive` that we're starting from the snapshot *remotepool/usr/home@tuesday* and creating a clone. The final argument gives the name of our clone, *remotepool/usr/wedshome*. We can now go into */remotepool/usr/wedshome* and make whatever changes we desire, without interfering with further replications.

Remember that creating this clone doesn't add the transmitted snapshot to the snapshots in the original destination, however. If we want to also create *remotepool/usr/home@wednesday*, we must retransmit it without the `-o origin` option.

Bookmarks

Snapshots can take up a lot of space, especially on a busy filesystem. If you have users building new software, downloading ISOs and then discarding them, and dumping core files everywhere, snapshots can get quite large. Unfortunately, incremental replications build off of snapshots. Bookmarks are a way to get around the need to retain your oldest snapshots, while still performing incremental replications.

An incremental replication doesn't need to know all of the blocks that have already been sent. It must know the birthtime of the youngest block already sent, so that it can send all younger blocks. A bookmark is a stripped-down snapshot, retaining only the birthtime of the newest block in the snapshot. You can use a bookmark as the starting point of an incremental replication.

Create a bookmark of the @friday snapshot of the weekday dataset. Bookmark names begin with a hash mark (#).

```
# zfs bookmark zroot/usr/home@friday \
     zroot/usr/home#bm-friday
```

View your bookmarks with `zfs list`.

```
# zfs list -t all -r mypool/weekday
NAME                        USED  AVAIL  REFER  MOUNTPOINT
zroot/usr/home              360K  13.5G    96K  /mypool/weekday
zroot/usr/home@monday        64K      -    96K  -
zroot/usr/home@tuesday       64K      -    96K  -
zroot/usr/home@wednesday     64K      -    96K  -
zroot/usr/home@thursday      64K      -    96K  -
zroot/usr/home@friday         8K      -    96K  -
zroot/usr/home#bm-friday      -       -      -  -
```

Now remove all of the snapshots from the source pool:

```
# zfs destroy -v zroot/usr/home@%
will destroy zroot/usr/home@monday
...
```

You now have only the bookmark left.

```
# zfs list -t all -r mypool/weekday
NAME                        USED  AVAIL  REFER  MOUNTPOINT
zroot/usr/home               96K  13.5G    96K  /mypool/weekday
zroot/usr/home#bm-friday      -       -      -  -
```

On Saturday, bake a fresh snapshot.

```
# zfs snapshot zroot/usr/home@saturday
```

```
# zfs list -t all -r zroot/usr/home
NAME                        USED  AVAIL  REFER  MOUNTPOINT
mypool/weekday               96K  13.5G    96K  /mypool/weekday
mypool/weekday@saturday       0       -    96K  -
mypool/weekday#bm-friday      -       -      -  -
```

Unhelpfully, bookmarks are listed after snapshots, even when they are older than the snapshots. The ZFS command line is very expressive, however. To make things easier, let's use `-t` to tell it to list only snapshots and bookmarks. The `-s` flag tells zfs(8) how to sort the output, so we'll sort by the `creation` (creation date) property. Add in a maximum recursion depth of *1* to ignore the snapshots of child datasets.

```
# zfs list -t snapshot,bookmark -s creation \
      -d 1 zroot/usr/home
NAME                        USED  AVAIL  REFER  MOUNTPOINT
zroot/usr/home#bm-friday      -       -      -  -
zroot/usr/home@saturday      64K      -    96K  -
```

Now replicate the @saturday snapshot to the remote host, using the `bm-friday` bookmark as the fromsnap.

```
# zfs send -i #bm-friday zroot/usr/home@saturday | \
    ssh hotspare zfs receive remotepool/backup/usrhome
```

The remote host captured the @saturday snapshot as an incremental snapshot, even though the source host no longer has Friday's snapshot.

```
# zfs list -t all -r remotepool/usrhome
NAME                                  USED  AVAIL  REFER  MOUNTPOINT
remotepool/backup/usrhome            58.5K   472M  19.5K  /remotepool/
weekday
remotepool/backup/usrhome@monday     9.50K      -  19.5K  -
remotepool/backup/usrhome@tuesday    9.50K      -  19.5K  -
remotepool/backup/usrhome@wednesday 9.50K      -  19.5K  -
remotepool/backup/usrhome@thursday  9.50K      -  19.5K  -
remotepool/backup/usrhome@friday        1K      -  19.5K  -
remotepool/backup/usrhome@saturday      0      -  19.5K  -
```

Bookmarks let us remove the snapshots from our source pool, saving space, but retain them on the destination pool so we can still refer back to old versions of files.

Resumable Send

Just because ZFS makes dataset replication simple, doesn't mean that the real world cooperates. As a dataset grows in size, chances increase that some transient network problem will break the connection and interrupt the stream. If you're almost done with a 40 GB data stream over the Internet, a two-minute outage at your ISP can spark some well-deserved rage. Don't go after the carrier with an axe; use resumable `zfs send` instead, letting you resume interrupted replications. Resumable `zfs send` first appeared in FreeBSD 10.3 in early 2016.

To make a ZFS stream resumable, add the `-s` flag to `zfs receive`.

The *mypool/from* dataset is a few gigabytes in size. By adding `-s` to the `zfs receive` statement, though, we make the stream resumable. Which is good, because we're going to interrupt the transmission with `CTRL-C`.

```
local# zfs snapshot mypool/from@resumeme
```

```
local# zfs send -v mypool/from@resumeme | \
      ssh hotspare zfs receive -s remotepool/to
full send of mypool/from@resumeme estimated size is 2.00G
total estimated size is 2.00G
TIME        SENT    SNAPSHOT
17:12:43    279M    mypool/from@resumeme
17:12:44    529M    mypool/from@resumeme
17:12:45    786M    mypool/from@resumeme
^C
```

Of course, because ZFS replication is unidirectional, the sender has no idea which blocks the recipient actually captured and wrote to the disk. Without resumable send, you'd have to start the whole transmission over again.

Over on the receiving host, the partially received dataset has a new property, **`receive_resume_token`**. The sender needs the value of this property to pick up where it left off.

```
remote# zfs get -H -o value receive_resume_token \
      remotepool/to
1-db9a171a3-c8-789c636064000310a500c4e-
c50360710e72765a5269740d80cd8e4d3d28a534b40320b-
4c61f26c48f2499525a9c540da20ecb02936fd25f9e9a599290c-
0cae0dba41478e981fb24092e704cbe725e6a6323014a5e6e-
697a416e4e7e7e8a715e5e73a14a51697e6a68264100000648b1d2c
```

Now provide that token to the sender with the `-t` flag. You do not need to include the source dataset, as the token includes everything `zfs send` requires. Adding the `-v` spills out more details about the transmission, though.

```
local# zfs send -v -t 1-db9a171a3-c8-789c636064000310a-
500c4ec50360710e72765a5269740d80cd8e4d3d28a534b40320b4c61f-
26c48f2499525a9c540da20ecb02936fd25f9e9a599290c0cae0d-
ba41478e981fb24092e704cbe725e6a6323014a5e6e697a416e4e7e7e-
8a715e5e73a14a51697e6a68264100000648b1d2c | zfs receive -s
remotepool/to
resume token contents:
nvlist version: 0
 object = 0x8
 offset = 0x35a00000
 bytes = 0x35c35630
 toguid = 0xc237c4c4522d8045
 toname = mypool/from@resumeme
full send of mypool/from@resumeme estimated size is 1.16G
TIME        SENT   SNAPSHOT
17:38:20    263M   mypool/from@resumeme
17:38:21    472M   mypool/from@resumeme
…
17:42:04   1.16G   mypool/from@resumeme
```

Once the `zfs receive` completes, the property becomes blank.

```
# zfs get receive_resume_token remotepool/to
NAME             PROPERTY               VALUE    SOURCE
remotepool/to    receive_resume_token   -        -
```

If you don't resume that send, the destination pool will have an unusable, incomplete dataset on it, taking up space better used by, well, anything. Delete that with `-A`.

```
remote# zfs receive -A remotepool/to
```

This removes the partially received stream and frees that space.

Automating Replication

Everybody wants backups, but backups that must be manually run are not backups—because they won't happen. Sure, you'll do them once or twice, but one day the coffee pot will break and you'll barely be able to remember where you left your spleen. Reliable backups demand automation and testing. Testing is always your problem, but for automation we have `zxfer`.

Zxfer(8) examines select local and remote datasets, determines which snapshots must be replicated to synchronize the two sets of data, and sends the datasets. It can also remove snapshots on the remote side once they're removed from the local pool.

FreeBSD does not include `zxfer` by default, but you can easily install it with `pkg`. As `zxfer` can work in both push and pull modes, you only need to install it on one of the systems. For our demonstration, we'll install it on both nodes.

```
# pkg install zxfer
```

The `zxfer` command does not currently support either bookmarks or resumable replication. It also doesn't set up replication user accounts. You must configure those accounts, create SSH keys, and set permissions exactly as you would for normal replication.

Using zxfer

All of our replication examples have used push mode; the host with the current datasets pushes them to a replication target. We'll start with using `zxfer` similarly. Enable push mode with `-T` and the login for the remote host.

Using `zxfer` requires that you declare if you want to replicate a single dataset, or the dataset and all its children. The `-R` flag enables recursion, while `-N` indicates a single dataset and its snapshots. For backups, recursive mode is almost always correct.

You might also add `-v`, for verbose mode.

```
$ zxfer -v -T user@host -R localpath remotepath
```

If the user account is the same on both sides, you can skip identifying the user.

One thing to remember is that arguments that take an argument of their own cannot be combined with arguments that don't require that. You can use `-v -T user@host`, but `-vT user@host` makes `zxfer` complain bitterly. (As `zxfer` is a shell script, it uses getopt(1) to handle command-line arguments, rather than the fancy option handling available in more complex languages.)

Here we replicate the *zroot/somedata* dataset to the pool *remotepool/backups* on the host **remote**.

```
local$ zxfer -T replicator@remote \
      -R mypool/somedata remotepool/backups
```

If you add the `-v` for verbose mode, you'll see `zxfer` transferring each snapshot.

```
Sending zroot/somedata@snappy to remotepool/backups/somedata.
Sending zroot/somedata@reply to remotepool/backups/somedata.
(incremental to zroot/somedata@snappy.)
Sending zroot/somedata@more to remotepool/backups/somedata.
(incremental to zroot/somedata@reply.)
```

Once `zxfer` exits, the host **remote** has all the snapshots.

```
remote$ zfs list -t all -r remotepool/backups/somedata
NAME                                  USED  AVAIL  REFER  MOUNTPOINT
remotepool/backups/somedata          10.1M  15.0G  10.1M  /remotepool/
backups/somedata
remotepool/backups/somedata@snappy      8K      -  10.1M  -
remotepool/backups/somedata@reply       8K      -  10.1M  -
remotepool/backups/somedata@more        8K      -  10.1M  -
```

Further replication on top of these snapshots can run either in push mode or in pull mode. Let's try pull mode next.

Zxfer Pull Mode

In pull mode, `zxfer` logs into the remote machine via SSH and runs `zfs send` to transfer snapshots back to the host running `zxfer`. Use the `-O` flag with the login and host to indicate pull mode. Everything else is the same.

```
$ zxfer -v -O user@host -R localpath remotepath
```

Now create an additional snapshot on the source host.

```
local$ zfs snapshot mypool/somedata@new
```

On the destination machine, run `zxfer` to pull the snapshots over. Here we're adding `-v` to show more detail of what really happens

```
remote# zxfer -v -O replicator@local \
      -R zroot/somedata remotepool/backups
Sending mypool/somedata@new to zroot/backups/somedata.
(incremental to zroot/somedata@more.)
```

The mounted dataset is updated with the new snapshot.

Rotating Snapshots

If you keep sending snapshots, eventually your remote pool will fill up. You probably want to destroy remote snapshots that no longer exist on the source machine. Use `-d` to accomplish this. Start by removing an old snapshot.

```
local# zfs destroy zroot/somedata@reply
```

Use the `-d` flag to prune any deleted snapshots from the destination:

```
local$ zxfer -vd -T remote \
      -R zroot/somedata remotepool/backup
```

In verbose mode, `zxfer` displays each dataset it destroys as well as those it creates.

```
Destroying destination snapshot
      remotepool/backup/somedata@reply.
```

You can watch as your hastily-typed incorrect command destroys your beloved data.

Keeping Old Snapshots

A common snapshot regimen calls for making snapshots every 15 minutes, and then every hour, day, week, and month. (We discuss such a rotation scheme in *FreeBSD Mastery: ZFS*.) The host discards 15-minute snapshots after a few hours, hourly snapshots after a couple days, and so on. You certainly want those 15-minute snapshots discarded on the remote host, but you might want the remote host to retain some snapshots even after the source destroys them. Many of us want to keep weekly or monthly snapshots as long-term backups.

The `-g` flag lets you protect the oldest backups with an argument of a number of days. For example, `-g 375` tells `zxfer` to not delete snapshots that are 375 days old or older.

Suppose you want to keep all the monthly snapshots, but automatically remove any other snapshots that get removed from the source. The source deletes monthly snapshots after three months, but weekly snapshots after six weeks. Six weeks is 42 days. Add an extra week for system anomalies, giving 49 days. Using a `-g` of 50 would tell `zxfer` to not delete any snapshot 50 days old or older.

```
local$ zxfer -vd -g 50 -T remote \
      -R zroot/somedata remotepool/backup
```

Eventually, your backup pool will fill up. You must go in and clean out the snapshots that are so old they're no longer useful. It's no different than cleaning out the corporate tape closet.

Properties and Disaster Recovery

You'll often want to replicate complex properties, like **sharenfs** and any of the quotas. The `-P` argument tells `zxfer` to set the properties in the destination to match the source.

In some cases you want to know what the properties are, but you don't want to restore them immediately upon replication. The `zxfer` command can copy dataset properties to a text file, letting you restore from that file later.

The `-k` flag tells `zxfer` to create the properties text file, in the root directory of the replica. The file is named *.zxfer_backup_info*, followed by a period and the pool name. If you're replicating an entire host web5's *zroot* pool to the *remotepool/web5* on the backup host, the properties backup file will be in *remotepool/web5/.zxfer_backup_info.zroot*.

Use the `-e` flag to restore the dataset and pool properties from this text file.

A common configuration is for a host to have a pool set aside to accept backups, and then a pool set aside for disaster recovery. If the source machine dies, you can use `zxfer` locally to copy the latest backup to the disaster-recovery pool. You'll find examples of exactly this in the zxfer(8) manual page, but here's a common example, including restoring properties. I'm restoring our backup of the host **web5**, into a pool also called *web5*.

```
# zxfer -deFPv -R remotepool/web5/ web5
```

Boot from the new *web5* pool, and you have restored service!

More Zxfer Options

The `zxfer` program has a bunch of options to copy with annoying situations.

If you have a complicated SSH setup, you might need to set some client options in the `zxfer` user's *$HOME/.ssh/config*. Alternatively, you could add these options in single quotes to `-O` and `-T`.

The `-O` and `-T` flags can also be used to inject SSH options, as well as command-line arguments. The additional parameters before the user and host get fed to SSH, while any commands after the user and host prefix the zfs(8) command. (You're better served configuring ZFS dataset permissions than using `sudo`, however.)

```
-O '-oPort=1022 -i /path/to/key/file \
     replication@hotspare sudo'
```

The `-F` flag tells `zfs receive` to roll back any datasets that block replication. If you've changed the replicated dataset, `-F` blows away those changes.

You can have `zxfer` take a snapshot automatically before running. It won't remove old snapshots, so it's not a proper snapshot rotation regimen. It works for immediate backups, however, leaving the problem of cleaning up for another day. Add the `-s` to have the `zxfer` take snapshots of every replicated dataset.

Finally, the `-n` flag triggers no-op mode. The `zxfer` program does not transfer or delete any snapshots. Instead, it performs its analysis and prints out what it would do if you hadn't set `-n`.

Now that you've gone through replication, the issues of ZFS volumes should seem easy in comparison. Or, maybe not…

Chapter 5: ZFS Volumes

A ZFS volume, or *zvol*, is a chunk of space backed by a ZFS pool and used as a block device. A zvol is normally used like a file-backed filesystem and exported to some other device by iSCSI. A zvol doesn't have the normal dataset files and directories and permissions, instead relying on whatever uses the volume to provide the filesystem. Zvols are commonly used as iSCSI targets for other network devices, giving you access to ZFS-backed storage on operating systems with less flexible filesystems. You can also use zvols as storage for virtual machines, giving any guest operating systems access to ZFS' integrity features even if the client operating system can't use ZFS. Plus, you can replicate zvols across the network.

We touched on zvols in *FreeBSD Mastery: ZFS*. This chapter exposes some common zvol pitfalls. But let's start with zvol basics.

Creating, Destroying, and Manipulating ZFS Volumes

The `-V` flag tells `zfs create` that you're making a ZFS volume. Give the desired size and the full path to the volume. Here we create a 2 TB zvol on the pool *vm*. As this volume will be exported to a web server, we'll name it *www1*.

```
# zfs create -V 2T vm/www1
```

Zvols must be the children of a dataset. In this example, the zvol is a child of the pool's root dataset. You cannot create a zvol as a child of a zvol. Our volume shows up in the list of datasets.

```
# zfs list -r vm
NAME      USED  AVAIL  REFER  MOUNTPOINT
vm       2.06T   563G  31.8K  /vm
vm/db1   2.06T  2.61T  15.9K  -
```

A zvol immediately claims all of the space you assigned for it. We created a 2 TB volume so it uses 2 TB of space plus some extra for metadata. A brand-new volume hasn't used this much space yet—it hasn't written a bunch of placeholder data to the pool or anything like that. It's only claimed that space via a refreservation.

Remove a volume with `zfs destroy`.

```
# zfs destroy vm/www1
```

You can use most other ZFS commands on zvols, such as renaming and moving. This volume is actually being used for data, so we give it a more meaningful name.

```
# zfs rename vm/www1 vm/db1
```

A zvol has many properties identical to other ZFS datasets, but not all. Zvols have unique properties such as **volmode** and **volblocksize**, while you can't set **sharenfs** or **atime** on a zvol.

Access a zvol through its device node. Most zvols have device nodes in */dev/zvol*, in a directory named after their pool. The device node for our sample zvol, *vm/db1*, would be */dev/zvol/vm/db1*. A zvol might have other device nodes, depending on its mode.

Sparse Volumes

ZFS lets you create a ZFS volume larger than the space available to stick it in, thus overcommitting on space. Reserving some space, but not enough, is called *thin provisioning*. Thin provisioning is quite risky on older filesystems, as you can easily provision more space than the filesystem contains. You can easily expand a ZFS pool by adding more hard drives, so it's not as much of a risk here. The **refreservation** property controls how much space a volume has reserved for it. Here we create the 2 TB zvol `db5`, but tell ZFS to reserve only 100 MB for it.

```
# zfs create -V 2T -o refreservation=100M db/db5
```

Those of us who have a couple of empty SAS shelves and already have plans for adding more hard drives might even use *sparse volumes.* Sparse volumes use only the amount of space used on the volume. Use the `-s` flag to create a sparse volume.

```
# zfs create -V 2T -s db/db5
```

You might use smaller reservations if you're exporting iSCSI volumes to other hosts and the client's filesystem is less flexible than ZFS. Growing an NTFS or UFS filesystem when the underlying disk expands can cause long-term problems. Using a sparse volume means you can tell the Windows host that an iSCSI device is a specific large size, even if the underlying pool doesn't have that much free space. The zvol supporting it consumes the amount of space used by the files on the device, plus any filesystem metadata.

This lets you create truly impressive volumes, if you're prepared to support them. Here we create a two exabyte sparse volume. It doesn't matter that the pool beneath it is only 500 GB.

```
# zfs create -V 2E -s db/db5
```

Use `gpart show /dev/zvol/db/db5`, and you'll see that this disk device really is two exabytes. If you truly need two exabytes of space on a single iSCSI volume, you can probably afford a flunky to unpack and mount hard drives quickly enough to keep up with demand.

Overcommitting gets really ugly when you run out of space. Your iSCSI clients might completely lose their cool when they're informed that these volumes are out of space even though the operating system instances insist that they're only 10 percent full. Many iSCSI stacks cope gracefully with such problems. Others… do not.

If you don't have enough physical hardware capacity to add storage, let ZFS volumes take up an amount of space equal to their size. Don't overcommit space.

Volume Mode

Before you go creating a volume for your application, consider its intended use and what hosts are going to access it. FreeBSD's default ZFS settings assume that the system hosting the zvol completely controls it. If you're using a zvol as a store for a virtual machine, however, the guest operating system expects to have complete control of it. This matters because FreeBSD's GEOM layer autoconfigures storage. Storage already configured by the host causes problems for virtualized guests.

Control which system configures a volume using the **`volmode`** property.

The default **`volmode`**, *geom*, means that the system where the volume exists controls it. If we create a zvol on host A, host A configures and manages the volume through GEOM. In addition to the device node for the ZFS volume, it gets device nodes in */dev/label* and such. Use the geom **`volmode`** when you're using a zvol locally.

The **`volmode`** *dev* means that this zvol is only available through the single device node in */dev/zvol*. GEOM doesn't try to autoconfigure this volume. You can assign a label to the node, but FreeBSD won't even try to see it. Use the dev **`volmode`** for virtual machine storage, such as bhyve(8) hosts.

The **`volmode`** *none* means that this zvol doesn't even get a device node. You could clone this volume, snapshot it, or replicate it. This mode is only useful for backups.

You can't change a live zvol's mode—while you can change the value of the **`volmode`** property, the volume's actual mode doesn't change.

To make a **volmode** change take effect, export and re-import the volume. (You could also rename the volume, which is effectively exporting the volume and importing it under a different name.)

Create volumes with the desired mode by specifying a mode at the command line or by setting a global default.

volmode at Command Line

As with any other property, use the `-o` flag to set the **volmode** when creating a zvol.

```
# zfs create -V 10G -o volmode=dev vm/swap0
```

This new zvol is accessible only by the device node *`/dev/zvol/vm/swap0`*.

Default volmode

If a host most commonly needs to use a **volmode** other than geom, it makes sense to change the default **volmode**. The sysctl vfs.zfs.vol.mode controls the default **volmode** for new zvols.

The default value, *1*, tells ZFS to use the **volmode** of geom. A setting of *2* indicates the dev **volmode**, while *3* means a **volmode** of none. Change the default with sysctl(8), or make the change permanently effective at the next reboot with an *`/etc/sysctl.conf`* entry. Here's an *`/etc/sysctl.conf`* entry to make a virtualization server create new zvols with a **volmode** of dev.

```
vfs.zfs.vol.mode=2
```

There's no need to explicitly define the geom **volmode**.

Accessing zvols

You can't `zfs mount` a zvol like you would a filesystem dataset. The whole point of a zvol is that it's a block device. To access it, you must access the device node or its GEOM provider. The most common is probably the device node.

A zvol gets a device node in */dev/zvol*, in a subdirectory named after the pool. The device node for our sample zvol, *vm/db1*, would be */dev/zvol/vm/db1*.

We might assign this zvol as storage for a `bhyve` virtual machine, in which case we'd probably let the virtual machine partition the disk.

For other uses we might want to partition it locally. Here we create a GPT partition scheme on the zvol and make it one large partition, with a GEOM label of *db1*. We also assign it a GEOM label.

```
# gpart create -s gpt /dev/zvol/vm/db1
zvol/vm/db1 created
# gpart add -t freebsd-ufs -l db1 /dev/zvol/vm/db1
zvol/vm/db1p1 added
# glabel create db1 /dev/zvol/vm/db1
```

As this zvol was created with the default **volmode**, geom, it's now also accessible through the device node */dev/label/db1*.

Once the partition exists you can create a filesystem on it.

```
# newfs -j /dev/zvol/vm/db1
/dev/zvol/vm/db1: 2097152.0MB (4294967296 sectors) block
size 32768, fragment size 4096
 using 3350 cylinder groups of 626.09MB, 20035 blks,
80256 inodes.
 with soft updates
...
```

Wait—why would we possibly want to use UFS on a zvol?

Perhaps our iSCSI client or VM guest doesn't have enough resources to run ZFS effectively. By giving the client a ZFS-backed volume with a filesystem it can support, the client gets the additional protections of ZFS even though the client can't use ZFS directly. I enable UFS soft updates journaling with `-j`, however, because ZFS data integrity and UFS filesystem journaling protect completely different things. ZFS integrity checks make sure that the writes are safe, but filesystem journaling verifies that all the writes are completed.[11]

Now that the zvol has a filesystem, you can mount it.

```
# mount /dev/gpt/db1 /media/
```

And voilà! I have a UFS filesystem backed by ZFS, ready for use.

The most common use for zvols is as backing stores for virtual machines. A serious quantity of virtual machines requires serious hardware. Let's take a look at that next.

11 Lucas has used a local USB flash drive as a gjournal(8) or gcache(8) cache for an iSCSI device. It worked. If you find yourself in a situation where that makes sense, however, leave the situation.

Chapter 6: Advanced Hardware

A typical server can only hold so many hard drives. As your storage needs grow, you'll eventually encounter more advanced hardware than you find on your typical home machine. This chapter covers enough of the basics to ensure that you know what your storage vendor is trying to sell you, and how to make use of these additional features.

SCSI Enclosure Services

The most common way to add storage is through a box specifically designed to hold hard drives. The most common is the SCSI enclosure (sometimes called a backplane). Attach a SCSI enclosure to a host with a disk controller card.

SCSI enclosures have all sorts of hardware and features in them. You'll often see SAS or SATA port multipliers, allowing you to connect more than four drives to each port on the disk controller. You'll probably see disk bays or trays, probably hot-swappable. An enclosure has fans, temperature sensors, power supplies, and more. An enclosure might even have its own CPU, running a custom operating system specifically designed to corral all of these features. Failed fans and power supplies can bring down your storage.

SCSI enclosures have protocols to communicate with server operating systems. SCSI Enclosure Services, or SES, is the modern protocol for monitoring and managing the storage subsystem of your server. It's the successor to the SCSI Accessed Fault-Tolerant Enclosure (SAF-TE) protocol found in older hardware.

SES is usually integrated into the backplane of the hot-swap bays or in the SAS Expander. SES provides a standard way to monitor and locate your disk drives, and can also be used to monitor fans, lights, and other devices.

FreeBSD supports SES with the ses(4) driver. FreeBSD 10.3 introduced sesutil(8), letting you examine and control the ses(4) devices on your system.

Examining your Enclosure

Sesutil(8) has many sub-functions. Start with `sesutil map`, which displays all of the devices in all of your enclosures.

```
# sesutil map
ses0:
 Enclosure Name: LSI SAS2X36 0e12
 Enclosure ID: 500304801786b87f
```

The first entry for an enclosure is the enclosure device name (ses0). If you have multiple controllers, a reboot might change the device node, so don't rely on it to identify a specific enclosure. The enclosure name is based on the hardware model, but the enclosure ID is unique to this particular piece of hardware.

Each piece of monitored or controlled hardware in an enclosure is an *element*. Each element is assigned a number. Element numbers do not change at reboot. Here's the first element of one of Jude's arrays.

```
Element 0, Type: Array Device Slot
 Status: Unsupported (0x00 0x00 0x00 0x00)
 Description: Drive Slots
```

Element 0 has the type *Array Device Slot*, and a description of *Drive Slots*. This is a parent element for all of the individual drive slots, which follow.

```
Element 1, Type: Array Device Slot
 Status: OK (0x01 0x00 0x00 0x00)
 Description: Slot 01
 Device Names: da0,pass4
Element 2, Type: Array Device Slot
 Status: OK (0x01 0x00 0x00 0x00)
 Description: Slot 02
 Device Names: da1,pass5
```

Here are a couple of actual hard drives. You'll see the FreeBSD device names and the drive's physical location. Presumably, your enclosure has slot numbers indelibly printed on it—preferably, not on the removable drive trays. When FreeBSD whines that disk da1 is dead, you can tell the on-site tech to go straight to Slot 02.

Other hardware appears after the drive bays.

```
Element 26, Type: Temperature Sensors
 Status: OK (0x01 0x00 0x39 0x00)
 Description: Temperature
 Extra status:
 - Temperature: 37 C
```

That's a lot of words to say that the first thermometer says the enclosure is at textbook body temperature.

```
Element 28, Type: Cooling
 Status: OK (0x01 0x01 0xfe 0x21)
 Description: Fan1
 Extra status:
 - Speed: 5100 rpm
```

A cooling element is probably a fan, although someone's probably built a supercooled SCSI enclosure by now. The fan speed lets you know the fan is still running. You might have to check the manual to see exactly where Fan1 is, though.

```
Element 34, Type: Voltage Sensor
 Status: OK (0x01 0x00 0x01 0xf6)
 Description: 5V
 Extra status:
 - Voltage: 5.02 V
```

The voltage sensors list each sensor's expected voltage as a *Description*, then provide the actual voltage as an extra status.

SAS expanders get a little more complex. You'll see entries for SAS expanders, and then all the components within the expander. There's very little to go wrong with a SAS expander, but some of the components do offer a status.

```
Element 41, Type: SAS Expander
 Status: Unsupported (0x00 0x00 0x00 0x00)
 Description: SAS Expanders
Element 42, Type: SAS Expander
 Status: OK (0x01 0x00 0x00 0x00)
 Description: Primary Expander
Element 44, Type: SAS Connector
 Status: OK (0x01 0x11 0xff 0x00)
 Description: Upstream Connector (Primary)
Element 45, Type: SAS Connector
 Status: OK (0x01 0x11 0xff 0x00)
 Description: Downstream Connector 1 (Primary)
Element 46, Type: SAS Connector
 Status: OK (0x01 0x11 0xff 0x00)
 Description: Downstream Connector 2 (Primary)
```

Even the individual connectors show up

```
Element 47, Type: SAS Connector
 Status: OK (0x01 0x20 0x00 0x00)
 Description: Drive Connector 00
```

This is far more detail than most of us need. But checking the status of your SAS expanders and controllers before you start replacing hard drives en masse can save you a lot of suffering.

Enclosure Path

You can describe a disk's location in an enclosure by how it's connected. To reach a particular disk, the operating system must go to a certain enclosure, then to a particular bay in that enclosure. FreeBSD automatically generates device node directories based on this path. This allows the sysadmin to identify the devices underlying a particular chunk of hardware. This device path is a series of key-value pairs, separated by `@` symbols. For example, enclosure 500304801786b87d shows up as enc@n500304801786b87d. Each path has four components: the enclosure, the device type, the slot, and then the element description, creating paths like the one below.

```
/dev/enc@n500304801786b87d/type@0/slot@a/elmdesc@Slot_10/
```

This device node represents enclosure 500304801786b87d. The leading *N* before the enclosure identifier shows that this is a Network Addressing Authority (NAA) identifier, which is largely vestigial because everything here is an NAA identifier. The hexadecimal number is the SAS address of the Addressed Logical Unit. How this number is determined varies by vendors.

The *type* is a numeric device type. Disks are the only devices this driver currently supports, but later FreeBSD versions might add support for other devices.

The *slot* is the drive bay. Slots are numbered in hexadecimal: slot a is 10, b is 11, and so on. Slot 10 is actually 16.

The last component is the *element description* that appears when you run `sesutil map`.

This directory contains symlinks to all of the device nodes associated with this slot. It even has label subdirectories. (You are managing your disks with labels, right?)

```
#ls -l /dev/enc@n500304801786b87d/type@0/slot@a/elmdesc@Slot_10/
total 1
lrwxr-xr-x  1 root  wheel   15 Oct  5 23:27 da9@ -> ../../../../da9
dr-xr-xr-x  2 root  wheel  512 Oct  5 23:27 gpt/
lrwxr-xr-x  1 root  wheel   18 Oct  5 23:27 pass13@ -> ../../../../pass13
```

If slot 15 on your enclosure is making an unusual buzzing noise, you can go into the enclosure-based device node and identify which providers live there.[12]

Keeping the lights on

The folks working on your hardware need all the help they can get. Those slot numbers are probably printed in six-point type, and only visible once you pull the drive out of the bay. And emergency drive replacements always happen when the on-site tech is barely conscious.

Enclosure bays have locate lights specifically to provide your remote hands an extra clue. Activate a bay's locate light with `sesutil locate`. Here, we activate the light on the bay housing drive da2.

```
# sesutil locate da2 on
```

The light either shines or blinks, depending on the manufacturer.

The `sesutil map` command shows if a slot's locate light is on.

```
# sesutil map
...
Element 3, Type: Array Device Slot
 Status: OK (0x01 0x00 0x02 0x00)
 Description: Slot 03
 Device Names: da2,pass6
 Extra status:
 - LED=locate
```

You might need to activate a locate light in a bay without a disk—say, to show the tech where to install a new hard drive. Use the SES device node and the element number rather than the device node. The slot number is often, but not always, the same as the element number. Be careful.

---

12 All sysadmins appreciate knowing exactly how much panic is appropriate at any given occasion.

Here we activate the locate light on element 3 on enclosure */dev/ses0*.

```
# sesutil locate -u /dev/ses0 3 on
```

To turn the locate light off, run the same command but replace *on* with … wait for it … *off*.

Controlling Host Bus Adapters

FreeBSD includes several tools for managing non-RAID hard drive controllers, normally called *host bus adapters*, or HBAs. For older controllers you probably would rather not be using any more, you'll find mfiutil(8) and mptutil(8). FreeBSD 10.3 adds the mprutil(8) and mpsutil(8) programs. Mprutil(8) is for the LSI Fusion-MPS 3 HBAs, while mpsutil(8) is for LSI Fusion-MPS 2 HBAs. (As Avago purchased LSI, you might also see these cards with Avago branding.)

Both programs behave identically, so we'll demonstrate with mpsutil(8).

Adapter Details

First, find the adapters connected to your system.

```
# mpsutil show adapters
Device Name  Chip Name   Board Name  Firmware
/dev/mps0    LSISAS2308              13000000
/dev/mps1    LSISAS2308              13000000
```

Now look at all of the devices attached. By default both tools access the first device node, either */dev/mps0* or */dev/mpr0*. Access other HBA devices with the *-u* flag and the device number.

```
# mpsutil show devices
B___T          SAS Address Handle Parent Device        Speed Enc  Slot Wdt
         500304801786b87f 0009   0001   SMP Target   6.0   0002 00   4
00  08   5000cca2325ddda9 000a   0009   SAS Target   6.0   0002 00   1
00  09   5000cca23257419d 000b   0009   SAS Target   6.0   0002 01   1
00  10   5000cca2325db3bd 000c   0009   SAS Target   6.0   0002 02   1
00  11   5000cca2325e028d 000d   0009   SAS Target   6.0   0002 03   1
...
```

Every line here is some device that responds to SCSI commands. The majority of them are hard drives. Anything that's on the SCSI bus is a target, including a hard drive. Really digging into this requires understanding of SAS and SCSI, but we can glean useful information without deep knowledge.

The first two columns show the device's SCSI-style address. The third gives the device's SAS address. Much like an Ethernet card, every SAS device has a unique physical address.

The *Handle* column indicates the name for the device, while the *Parent* column shows what device this device is attached to. Look at our first line. It has a handle of 0009. The second column has a handle of 000a, but its parent is 0009. The device on line two is attached to the device on line one.

The *Device* column shows what kind of device this is. A "SAS Target" is a fancy way of saying "a SAS hard drive." An SMP (Serial Attached Management Protocol) target is a SAS switch or expander.

The *Speed* column shows the connection speed in gigabytes per second.

The *Enc* column shows the enclosure, while the *Slot* column shows the slot or drive bay. Finally, the *Wdt* column shows the maximum number of port connections on this device.

Display Enclosures

Use the `show enclosures` command to view the enclosures attached to an HBA. Here we list the enclosures connected to */dev/mps1*.

```
# mpsutil -u 1 show enclosures
Slots Logical ID      SEPHandle  EncHandle Type
  08  500605b009d018c0           0001      Direct Attached SGPIO
  25  500304801786b87f  0022     0002      External SES-2
  13  5003048001f7ab3f  0030     0003      External SES-2
```

You'll see the number of slots in the enclosure, the device's handle (if any), and the type of enclosure.

The *Logical ID* is a SAS address. You can map these to SAS addresses shown in sesutil(8) or other commands.

sas2ircu

If you are using an older version of FreeBSD that doesn't have `mpsutil`, or need functionality that it doesn't provide, LSI/Avago provides their own proprietary tool, sas2ircu(8). Most of the features mpsutil(8) lacks involve the controller's built-in software RAID.[13] Sas2ircu(8) also lets you get information like the HBA's firmware version. It's available as a FreeBSD port, sysutils/sas2ircu.

The sas2ircu(8) program expects at least two arguments: a controller (device node) number and a command. Even if you have only one controller, you must specify the controller number.

Viewing Hardware

To see the hardware attached to an HBA, use the display command. Here we look at the devices attached to controller 0, */dev/mps0* or */dev/mpr0*.

```
# sas2ircu 0 display
```

You'll get a bunch of copyright information, as well as helpful notes like this:

```
Read configuration has been initiated for controller 0
```

Or, "I'm going to do as you asked now."

13 You're not trying to use software RAID underneath ZFS, are you? Don't make Jude come down there!

```
----------------------------------
Controller information
----------------------------------
  Controller type          : SAS2308_2
  BIOS version             : 7.37.00.00
  Firmware version         : 19.00.00.00
  Channel description      : 1 Serial Attached SCSI
...
```

BIOS and firmware versions are useful if you have to troubleshoot or use the manufacturer's technical support. Once all this is past, we get information on the actual hardware. Each hard drive gets an entry like this.

```
Physical device information
---------------------------------------------------
Initiator at ID #0

Device is a Hard disk
  Enclosure #                  : 1
  Slot #                       : 0
  SAS Address                  : 4433221-1-0300-0000
  State                        : Ready (RDY)
  Size (in MB)/(in sectors)    : 4769307/9767541167
  Manufacturer                 : ATA
  Model Number                 : TOSHIBA MD04ACA5
  Firmware Revision            : FP2A
  Serial No                    : 55FGK5SUFS9A
  GUID                         : N/A
  Protocol                     : SATA
  Drive Type                   : SATA_HDD
...
```

You see serial numbers, the drive type, if the drive is ready to use or not, the size, and more.

Once you get through all of the hard drives, it'll spill out details about the enclosure itself.

```
------------------------------------
Enclosure information
------------------------------------
  Enclosure#  : 1
  Logical ID  : 500605b0:09cfc820
  Numslots    : 8
  StartSlot   : 0
------------------------------------
```

It's not quite everything about your enclosure—it won't tell you which drive is responsible for that burning smell—but it provides guidance.

sas2ircu Locate Lights

To turn the LED on a specific drive bay on or off, you'll need the controller number, the enclosure number, and the slot number. Get all that from the display command.

```
# sas2ircu <controller #> locate <enclosure#:slot#> on
```

Suppose we want to activate the LED on drive 8 on the enclosure shown in the previous section. We were using controller 0, or */dev/mps0*. The display command shows each device's enclosure number and slot number. Drive 8 is in slot 7—remember, slots often start numbering at zero. So to blink the LED for drive 8 (above) on */dev/mps0*, you would run.

```
# sas2ircu 0 locate 1:7 on
```

Turn it off again when you're done.

SAS Multipath

Systems with high availability requirements and many disks might need *SAS Multipath*. The goal of multipath is to provide more than a single path from the CPU to each disk. The other paths can be used for load balancing or failover. Generally, multipath means connecting two or more controllers to the backplane or storage shelf that contains the disks.

Why Multipath?

When each disk can be reached via any of the controllers, the failure of one controller or cable doesn't have to interrupt service. Additionally, it can allow you to use the combined bandwidth of all of the controllers.

This concept can even be extended to provide full High Availability. If you have a JBOD shelf full of disks, connect one of the two SAS ports to the first server, and the other to the second server. Now both machines have access to the disks. Use something like CARP, one of the many heartbeat daemons, or some quorum-based high availability service to allow these two servers to share an IP address.

With both machines having access to all the data, you can gracefully fail over services between the machines. This lets you do that OS upgrade you have been putting off, without taking down the file server.

Take extra care to ensure that both systems don't try to mount the disks simultaneously. This is why the `zpool import` command checks the Host ID, and refuses to import pools that look like they're in use by another system.

Multipath Modes

Multipath poses an interesting problem. If each of your disks has two or more paths back to the CPU, the operating system sees each individual disk multiple times, once via each controller. Now my 36-disk system suddenly appears to have 72 disks.

The GEOM multipath module, gmultipath(8), takes these multiple paths and provides a single logical storage device to the operating system. Gmultipath(8) automatically chooses the best path to reach the disk, so the upper storage layers don't have to worry about it.

GEOM multipath currently supports three modes of operation: active/passive, active/active, and active/read.

Active/passive uses only one path at a time. When a path fails, the system reissues the command on the next path. Specify active/passive with `-P`.

Active/active mode uses all paths simultaneously to increase the available bandwidth. Using all the paths can sometimes actually hurt performance. The active/active mode has no idea what's happening at the filesystem or application level; it just sprays the instructions across the different controllers. Commands that depend on each other might have to wait for a response from the other controller before they are able to proceed. Specify active/active mode with `-A`.

Active/read mode uses all paths for reads, but does all writes via the primary path. This hybrid approach resolves some of the write order problems that can be introduced by using active/active mode. This mode may help saturate an SSD by providing more controller bandwidth. On a regular spinning disk, random I/O performance may actually be worse than active/passive. Specify active/read with `-R`.

A fourth mode, *logical block*, is being investigated, but is not available yet. Logical block mode breaks the disk up into chunks of a specified size, and always uses the same path to access that region. This can avoid cache duplication on the controllers, as the same region of the disk will not be accessed by both controllers. This can also solve the write ordering issue and is expected to provide better performance than active/active mode.

Identifying Disks

The annoying part of configuring multipath is identifying which devices nodes (*/dev/daX*) represent different views of the same hardware. You must solve this before you add any labels to the disks. One way to solve this is to use camcontrol(8) on SAS devices to get the serial number.

```
# camcontrol inquiry da7 -S
  1EHNLWRC
# camcontrol inquiry da43 -S
  1EHNLWRC
```

Compile a list of devices and their serial numbers, and find the ones that match up.

Alternatively, you can use sesutil(8) to match up slot numbers. We'll use Jude's multipath system as an example. It has two enclosures: the front one has 24 slots, and the rear one 12. The server has two disk controllers.

The first controller's first port is plugged into the front enclosure, and gets called */dev/ses0*. The second port is plugged into the rear enclosure, and becomes */dev/ses1*.

The second controller's first port is plugged into the front enclosure, and gets assigned */dev/ses2*. The second controller's second port gets attached to the rear enclosure's second port, and becomes */dev/ses3*.

You have two enclosures. FreeBSD's */dev/ses0* and */dev/ses2* both point to the front enclosure, while */dev/ses1* and */dev/ses3* both point to the rear. Here I look at the front array's element 8 from both perspectives.

```
# sesutil map -u /dev/ses0
...
Element 8, Type: Array Device Slot
  Status: OK (0x01 0x00 0x00 0x00)
  Description: Slot 08
  Device Names: da7,pass11
# sesutil map -u /dev/ses2
...
Element 8, Type: Array Device Slot
  Status: OK (0x01 0x00 0x00 0x00)
  Description: Slot 08
  Device Names: da43,pass49
```

This is the same disk. It has multiple device nodes. Disks da7 and da43 are the same piece of hardware.

Any time you configure multipath, take notes and draw pictures. Future You will thank you for good notes.[14]

Configuring multipath

Gmultipath(8) needs a kernel module. Enable it at boot with a */boot/loader.conf* entry.

```
geom_multipath_load="YES"
```

The FreeBSD GEOM multipath modules have two configuration modes: manual and automatic. Automatic mode is highly recommended. It writes a label to the last sector of the disk, then reads that label via each path to determine which device nodes are just additional paths to the same disk. Use the gmultipath label to automatically configure multipath.

We advise using sesutil(8) to get the list of drive device nodes attached to one of your enclosures. Then use camcontrol(8) to get the serial number of each of those drives. Combine the enclosure (*f* for front) and slot number with the disk serial number to create a label on the disk.

```
# gmultipath label f01-1EHNM9MC /dev/da0
```

You'll run this once for each drive in the enclosure, using the slot number and serial number to create unique labels on each disk.

```
# gmultipath label f08-1EHNLWRC /dev/da7
```

Once the label exists, gmultipath(8) finds the label when it tastes the other disks. When it finds the disk with the gmultipath label f01-1EHNM9MC, it says "A-ha! This is the same as disk */dev/da0*" and takes over.

14 If your notes are poor or nonexistent, Future You will curse you, the day you were born, and your pets. Don't enough people hate you already?

Multipath Device Nodes

Now that you've mapped */dev/da0* and */dev/da37* to the same device, don't use those device nodes. These device nodes represent accessing the disk over a single path. Use the multipath device node instead. The gmultipath(8) kernel module actually prevents you from accessing those device nodes separately.

Multipath device nodes appear in */dev/multipath*. Each disk is named after the label you assigned. Build your ZFS array on top of these labels, and you'll get access to the disk even when you unplug a cable.

If you really, really want to access the multiple device nodes of a multipath device, set the sysctl kern.geom.multipath.exclusive to *0*. But we're telling you not to.[15]

Manual Multipath Configuration

Maybe you like doing things the hard way. If you have a handy chart of which device nodes represent the same physical device, you can use that chart to create multipath nodes by hand. Use `gmultipath create` to manually configure multipath devices. Provide a label and the two disk devices. Here we create the multipath device `multi1`, using device nodes `/dev/da7` and `/dev/da43`.

```
# gmultipath create multi1 /dev/da7 /dev/da43
```

To destroy a manually created multipath device, use `gmultipath destroy` and the label name.

```
# gmultipath destroy multi1
```

We really do recommend automatic configuration, though. And labeling disks after their location and serial number.

15 We're telling you not to for your own good, and not just so we can say "we told you so" later.

Viewing Multipath

After a reboot, FreeBSD's GEOM stack tastes the disks, recognizes the labels, and groups the disks together. See what it's discovered with `gmultipath status`.

```
# gmultipath status
                    Name   Status  Components
multipath/f00-1EHNM9MC  OPTIMAL  da0 (ACTIVE)
                                 da36 (PASSIVE)
multipath/f01-1EHJZMBC  OPTIMAL  da1 (ACTIVE)
                                 da37 (PASSIVE)
...
multipath/f07-1EHNLWRC  OPTIMAL  da7 (ACTIVE)
                                 da43 (PASSIVE)
```

After each path, you'll see a note indicating whether each device node is active or passive.

Changing Multipath Mode

We discussed the different multipath modes and their performance impacts earlier. Gmultipath defaults to active/passive (`-P`) when you label a disk. You can add the `-A` to trigger active/active, or `-R` to switch to active/read.

You can also use these flags to change the mode of an existing multipath device. Use `gmultipath configure`, the flag for the desired mode, and the drive's gmultipath label. Here we switch the disk labeled f07-1EHNLWRC to active/read mode.

```
# gmultipath configure -R f07-1EHNLWRC
```

Did it work?

```
# gmultipath status
...
multipath/f07-1EHNLWRC  OPTIMAL  da7 (ACTIVE)
                               da43 (READ)
```

In active/passive and active/read configurations, you can also use the `rotate` command to switch which of the devices is active.

```
# gmultipath rotate f07-1EHNLWRC
# gmultipath status
…
multipath/f07-1EHNLWRC  OPTIMAL  da7 (READ)
                                 da43 (ACTIVE)
```

Now, even your SSDs can rotate. Enjoy!

Speaking of SSDs…

SSDs

Solid state disks, or *SSDs*, are significantly different than regular spinning drives, and require tuning utterly different from traditional disks. For one thing, they're not even disks.

For a spinning hard drive to read two sectors that reside at different locations on the disk, the read head must position itself in the right location, then wait for the spinning platter to come around to the correct location, read the sector, then reposition itself to the second sector, again wait for the platter to come around to the correct offset, then read the second sector. This waiting is called the *seek time.*

An SSD has no moving parts. When you read data from two different parts of the drive, the drive has a seek time of zero. Most SSDs get their relatively high read and write speeds from the fact that they read and write to multiple cells concurrently. In order to keep multiple memory cells busy, the operating system must supply the drive with a queue of work to complete.

For a normal spinning drive, having a "deep" queue is bad. It means the amount of time between when data is requested and when it is written or returned is higher, because it must wait for the work ahead of it in the queue to complete. By having a lower queue depth, more important work items can get to the front of the queue first, cutting in front of less important work that has been patiently waiting in line[16]. To get the most out of an SSD, however, the queue depth must

16 Almost as skillfully as Lucas cuts in line at the gelato stand.

be high enough to make sure each cell gets assigned work. You cannot get the performance numbers boasted on the box without a nice full queue.

To get the most out of a high IOPS device like an SSD, the ZFS VDEV queue depth tunable probably needs increasing. This helps keep enough work in the queue to prevent the device from being idle. See the “I/O Queues” section of Chapter 8.

Unlike a spinning disk, which has sectors that reside at fixed locations on the platter, SSDs are an array of immobile flash cells. SSDs use an FTL[17] (Flash Translation Layer) to map the emulated locations on disk to the particular flash cell containing stored data. While SSDs claim to have the Logical Block Addresses used by spinning disks, the FTL provides these LBAs. LBAs on an SSD bear even less relationship to reality than they do on spinning disks.

Since flash cells wear out, almost all SSDs contain more storage than they claim on the box. The drives spread data around the cells in order to wear them more evenly. Once all of the space is occupied, a garbage collector runs. The garbage collector finds cells that are no longer referenced, or which the OS has used the TRIM (SATA) or UNMAP (SCSI) command to mark as unused, and clears them for further use.

When you add SSDs or other devices that support TRIM to a ZFS pool, FreeBSD TRIMs the entire partition or device by default, so that it starts in a known state. This can cause a delay of tens of minutes or even hours before the drive is usable. If your devices are new, or you do not want to TRIM them when you add them to the pool, set the sysctl vfs.zfs.vdev.trim_on_init to *0* before adding the device to the pool.

17 Sadly, not a Faster Than Light engine.

NVMe

Non-Volatile Memory Express, or *NVMe*, is a newer technology designed to further increase solid state storage speed. It's used for flash drives, as well as other non-volatile memory like Intel's 3D Xpoint. NVMe itself is a physical interface specification, an alternative to SATA or SCSI/SAS. You'll find NVMe cables and adapters that attach via the PCI-e bus.

The slowest, most complicated, and most error-prone part of an SSD is the FTL. Pretending to be as stupid as a 1980s-era spinning disk is hard labor. NVMe improves performance on the same hardware by dropping this clumsy pretense, instead adopting protocols better suited for flash memory.

One of the biggest differences between NVMe devices and SSDs is that NVMe devices have multiple queues, usually one read and one write queue per CPU. Rather than trying to try to keep a single queue full of enough work to occupy multiple flash cells, NVMe has multiple queues. NVMe queues can be kept relatively shallow, to allow high-priority tasks to supersede other work. Spreading the load across CPUs helps ensure even greater performance.

While most HDDs and SSDs interface with AHCI, which has a single command queue of up to 64 commands per device, the NVMe interface allows 65,536 queues, of 65,536 commands each. The NVMe interface thus requires less locking while offering far greater parallelism and therefore performance.

FreeBSD's nvme(4) driver first appeared in FreeBSD 9.2. Much like a hard drive device node, you can expect the first nvme(4) device to be `/dev/nvme0`, `/dev/nvme1`, and so on.

NVMe devices natively support *namespaces*, allowing them to be divided up into logical units, similar but different to partitioning. Nvme(4) uses the characters *ns* to identify namespaces in the device node. Unlike most everything else in computing, the NVM Express specification starts numbering namespaces at 1 rather than 0. You'll thus get device nodes like */dev/nvme0ns1*, */dev/nvme0ns2*, and so on.

Only some newer Enterprise NVMe devices support managing the namespaces. Most current devices have a single namespace that covers the entire device.

Viewing NVMe Devices

Use nvmecontrol(8) to manage NVMe devices. Start by identifying all of the NVMe hardware connected to the system with `nvmecontrol devlist`.

```
# nvmecontrol devlist
 nvme0: INTEL SSDPEDMD800G4
  nvme0ns1 (763097MB)
```

This host has a single NVME, with a single namespace.

Use the `nvmecontrol identify` command to learn specific information about the device.

```
# nvmecontrol identify nvme0
Controller Capabilities/Features
================================
Vendor ID:                  8086
Subsystem Vendor ID:        8086
Serial Number:              CVFT4030004A800CGN
Model Number:               INTEL SSDPEDMD800G4
Firmware Version:           8DV10151
...
```

This goes on for quite a bit, identifying all of the features this NVMe supports (or doesn't).

The `identify` command also works on the namespaces.

```
# nvmecontrol identify nvme0ns1
Size (in LBAs):               1562824368 (1490M)
Capacity (in LBAs):           1562824368 (1490M)
Utilization (in LBAs):        1562824368 (1490M)
Thin Provisioning:            Not Supported
Number of LBA Formats:        7
Current LBA Format:           LBA Format #00
LBA Format #00: Data Size:   512  Metadata Size:   0
LBA Format #01: Data Size:   512  Metadata Size:   8
LBA Format #02: Data Size:   512  Metadata Size:  16
LBA Format #03: Data Size:  4096  Metadata Size:   0
LBA Format #04: Data Size:  4096  Metadata Size:   8
LBA Format #05: Data Size:  4096  Metadata Size:  64
LBA Format #06: Data Size:  4096  Metadata Size:   128
```

The LBA format allows you to specify the sector size, including optional extra space for encryption or metadata. FreeBSD does not yet let you reformat the drive with different sector sizes, however.

NVMe Performance

The nvmecontrol(8) utility also includes a performance testing tool, `nvmecontrol perftest`. While you might want to test the performance of a drive, it can demonstrate the advantages of multiple work queues.

Here we use the performance test to measure reading speed with an increasing number of threads, each for 30 seconds. Each test uses an increasingly large block sizes. The last column shows the actual throughput for each number of threads, in megabytes per second.

Start with 512-byte blocks.

```
# for threads in 1 2 4 8 16 32 64; do nvmecontrol perftest \
      -n $threads -o read -s 512 -t 30 nvme0ns1;done
Threads:  1 Size:   512  READ Time:  30 IO/s:  215377 MB/s:  105
Threads:  2 Size:   512  READ Time:  30 IO/s:  309203 MB/s:  150
Threads:  4 Size:   512  READ Time:  30 IO/s:  509559 MB/s:  248
Threads:  8 Size:   512  READ Time:  30 IO/s:  534976 MB/s:  261
Threads: 16 Size:   512  READ Time:  30 IO/s:  535131 MB/s:  261
Threads: 32 Size:   512  READ Time:  30 IO/s:  534682 MB/s:  261
Threads: 64 Size:   512  READ Time:  30 IO/s:  533701 MB/s:  260
```

With one thread, we can read 105 MB/s. With eight or more, we hit 260 MB/s. That's probably the maximum throughput with this block size on this device.

Here's the same test using 4096-byte (4 KB) reads.

```
# for threads in 1 2 4 8 16 32 64; do nvmecontrol perftest \
      -n $threads -o read -s 4096 -t 30 nvme0ns1;done
Threads:  1 Size:   4096  READ Time:  30 IO/s:  171261 MB/s:  668
Threads:  2 Size:   4096  READ Time:  30 IO/s:  308112 MB/s: 1203
Threads:  4 Size:   4096  READ Time:  30 IO/s:  424894 MB/s: 1659
Threads:  8 Size:   4096  READ Time:  30 IO/s:  521704 MB/s: 2037
Threads: 16 Size:   4096  READ Time:  30 IO/s:  543984 MB/s: 2124
Threads: 32 Size:   4096  READ Time:  30 IO/s:  543376 MB/s: 2122
Threads: 64 Size:   4096  READ Time:  30 IO/s:  542464 MB/s: 2119
```

Even at one thread, we blow away the performance possible with 512-byte blocks. Eight threads can do about 2,000 MB/s, while at 16 and more we get about 2120 MB/s. With a bit more testing, you could figure out that somewhere around nine or ten threads maximizes performance with this block size.

Now forget these puny mortal block sizes, and jump up to 128 KB blocks.

```
Threads:  1 Size: 131072  READ Time:  30 IO/s:   21770 MB/s: 2721
Threads:  2 Size: 131072  READ Time:  30 IO/s:   25780 MB/s: 3222
Threads:  4 Size: 131072  READ Time:  30 IO/s:   25780 MB/s: 3222
Threads:  8 Size: 131072  READ Time:  30 IO/s:   25758 MB/s: 3219
Threads: 16 Size: 131072  READ Time:  30 IO/s:   25706 MB/s: 3213
Threads: 32 Size: 131072  READ Time:  30 IO/s:   25718 MB/s: 3214
Threads: 64 Size: 131072  READ Time:  30 IO/s:   25710 MB/s: 3213
```

Two threads maximizes throughput with these large blocks.

A mere 3200 MB/s might not sound fast—it's 3.2 GB/s. But SATA measures performance in bits, not bytes. Once you get rid of the overhead, SATA 3's 6 GB/s maxes out at about 550 MB/s.

NVMe GEOM Providers and Booting

Once an NVMe device has a namespace, the nvd(4) driver comes into play. This is the device that is actually a GEOM provider, and can be used for storing data with ZFS. You'll see device nodes like */dev/nvd0*, */dev/nvd1*, and so on.

If you plan to use the NVMe device as a boot drive you must partition the boot */dev/nvd* device, probably with GPT. If you're not booting from the device, you could skip the partition table and write the filesystem directly on the device node.

Traditional BIOS and CSM modules only understand traditional disks and things that lie to look like them. The whole point of NVMe devices is that they refuse to lie, and do not emulate a traditional hard drive.

Booting from an NVMe device requires booting with UEFI. FreeBSD gained the ability to boot root-on-ZFS via EFI in FreeBSD 10.3.

zfsd

FreeBSD 11.0, expected to be released in July 2016, will include the first version of zfsd(8). This daemon, specific to FreeBSD, offers some of the functionality provided by Solaris' Fault Management Architecture (FMA). Zfsd(8) receives notifications about faults that the kernel cannot handle itself, and resolves them.

The daemon listens for devctl(4) events such as I/O errors or disk attach and removal events, then responds to them by activating and deactivating hot spares, or onlining and offlining individual devices in the pool.

Zfsd(8) does not require any configuration. It makes all of its decisions based on your pool configuration. In the first version of `zfsd`, only the **`autoreplace`** pool property has any effect.

If a device removal notification is received for a disk that is a member of a VDEV, `zfsd` immediately activates a hot spare in the pool and starts resilvering.

When a new GEOM device appears, `zfsd` first checks for a ZFS label. If the disk has a label that indicates it was previously a member of a pool, it is reattached. Once it finishes resilvering, any hot spares that were temporarily replacing that device are deactivated and returned to the list of available spares.

If the newly arrived device has no ZFS label, but its physical path matches that of a missing member of a VDEV, and the pool has the **`autoreplace`** pool property set, then the new device is used to replace the missing one. In newer FreeBSD versions the physical path might be blank, or it might be the SES path, like *`/dev/enc@n500304801786b87d/type@0/slot@1/elmdesc@Slot_01/gpt/f01-1EHJZMBC`*.

Once resilvering completes, `zfsd` deactivates any hot spares that were temporarily replacing that device. Deactivated devices get returned to the list of available spares.

If a VDEV becomes degraded or faulted, `zfsd` attempts to resolve the issue by activating a hot spare.

If an individual device generates more than 50 I/O or checksum errors in a 60-second period, `zfsd` marks the device as degraded and activates a hot spare. ZFS continues to use the degraded device while the pool resilvers. Once the pool finishes resilvering, `zfsd` removes the failing device from the pool.

If a new hot spare is added, or returned, to the pool, `zfsd` activates the spare if it is needed to replace another device.

When a resilver operation completes, `zfsd` attempts to deactivate any hot spares that are no longer needed, so that they are available to replace further failures should they occur.

Zfsd(8) also listens for "physical path change" events, to be notified when the path to a newly arriving disk is set. This can happen slightly later than when the disk insert event itself arrives. When the physical path is updated, and the pool's **`autoreplace`** property is set, `zfsd` attempts to replace any missing disk with the same physical path.

When you swap out a failed disk, and the CAM subsystem notes that the new disk is in the same slot, with the same path, `zfsd` automatically initiates the `replace` operation and restores the pool back to a healthy state.

Moving a disk from one slot to another works exactly like removing a disk and plugging a disk back in. The kernel marks an absent disk as removed. When you put the disk back in, the kernel sees the ZFS label on the disk, identifies which pool it belongs to, and automatically reactivates it with `zpool online`. The pool metadata gets updated with the physical path.

Now that we've talked some about how to use advanced hardware, let's look at advanced uses of the various ZFS caches.

Chapter 7: Caches

Like any other filesystem, ZFS uses in-memory caches to enhance performance. Unlike most other filesystems, though, the sysadmin can tweak these caches to adjust system behavior. ZFS caches a list of system pools in the `zpool.cache` file. It can use cache devices for reading and writing. The most visible cache, though, is ZFS's Adaptive Replacement Cache.

Adaptive Replacement Cache

Calling data from memory is much faster than accessing files from disk. Unix-like operating systems normally retain copies of the most recently accessed files in an in-memory buffer cache. ZFS uses a more sophisticated and more effective type of cache, the Adaptive Replacement Cache, or *ARC*. Understanding the ARC starts with understanding the buffer cache.

Traditional Buffer Cache

The buffer cache chooses data to cache based on the Least Recently Used, or *LRU*, algorithm. The LRU is a list, stored by the last time a chunk of data was accessed. Whenever an object is used, it moves to the top of the list. When the cache fills up, the system drops items from the bottom of the list until there's enough room to insert new items at the top of the list.

Buffer caches work well enough to provide performance gains, but in certain situations the LRU method causes undesirable behavior.

Consider a nightly backup. The backup program scans the entire hard drive, looking for files modified since the last backup. Running this scan adds each file on the system to the top of the list, letting files that were just scanned fall off the bottom. By the end of the backup, the buffer cache is full of data that nobody cares about. Meanwhile, the mission-critical database has been shoved entirely to disk. This is called *cache thrashing*.

The ARC avoids these problems.

ARC Design

The ARC also caches files that have been recently read from disk. Instead of a single list, the ARC has two pairs of lists. One is the Most Recently Used, or *MRU*, list, tracking accessed filesystem blocks much like the buffer cache. The second is the Most Frequently Used (MFU) list, tracking filesystem blocks that get used regularly.

The addition of the MFU list reduces the impact of cache-thrashing processes like the hypothetical backup job. While scanning every file on the system purges the MRU list, it won't affect the MFU list. Scanning a block once, for backup purposes, is not "frequent." The most frequently used files remain cached in memory. Running your backup still impacts disk I/O, reducing write performance, but the system serves the most popular files from the copy cached in memory.

Each list is paired with a *ghost* list, which contains the information about blocks that have been evicted from the list. When the MRU or MFU lists fill up, the blocks at the bottom of the list fall off. By tracking these blocks dropped from the caches, the ARC can prevent a block from constantly cycling in and out of the cache. The ARC can also decide if a block is now being used frequently enough to warrant entry onto the MFU list.

In almost all cases, the ARC is self-adjusting and a sysadmin's manual tuning can only impair performance. It's possible that your particular application might need special handling. Understand how the ARC behaves before you start fiddling with it, however.

ARC Memory Use

The ARC is designed to be both greedy and generous. If the system has free memory, and the ARC thinks it might possibly benefit from it, the ARC claims the memory. Every time the system reads something from disk, the ARC caches the file in memory. The ARC continues caching files until the system is using all of its memory.

FreeBSD reserves 1 GB of RAM for the kernel and application programs. All the rest of the system memory is fair game for the ARC. On a long-running system with a lot of storage and not a lot of memory, it's not surprising to see the ARC consume a majority of the system memory.

The ARC has a very low priority for memory requests, however. If an application requests memory, but the system doesn't have free memory, the kernel shrinks the ARC to give the application its requested memory. The process of returning memory from the ARC to the system as free member is not instantaneous; it can take a few seconds.

So: if the memory is free, the ARC will use it. If something needs that memory, the ARC gives it back. Modern servers have a lot of memory. They might as well use it for something. The old saying "Free RAM is wasted RAM" still holds true.

The easiest way to check the size of the ARC is through top(1). Here's a slice of `top` output from a fileserver with 32 GB of RAM and 20 TB of disk.

...

```
Mem: 168M Active, 116M Inact, 24G Wired, 1168K Cache,
449M Buf, 7052M Free
ARC: 23G Total, 15G MFU, 7398M MRU, 18K Anon,
412M Header, 88M Other
...
```

The *Mem* line appears in top output on almost all Unix-like systems, and offers details into how much memory the system is using for various types of tasks. While the ARC is a subset of wired memory, the ARC appears separately so it can offer more detail.

The first entry, *Total*, shows how much RAM the ARC is using. This ARC on this system has claimed a total of 23 GB.

Files that ZFS accesses often appear in the *MFU* space. This shows 15 GB of MFU data in the ARC.

The *MRU* entry shows 7,398 MB used to store the most recently accessed files.

Data moving from one queue to another, or async writes waiting to be flushed to disk, appear in the *Anon* space. Memory listed as *Header* is used for metadata about the ARC itself. This 23 GB of ARC needs 412 MB of metadata. *Other* includes things like runtime-only metadata used to help the ARC find stuff in its cache. Strictly speaking, it's not part of the cache itself, but supporting infrastructure.

While the ARC is greedy for RAM, note that this long-running system still has several gigabytes of free memory. The disks are overwhelmingly full, but the amount of data demanded by real users is comparatively small. Anyone who's managed a file server recognizes this pattern—every business' accounting department has one master spreadsheet, plus 15 bajillion slightly different copies of that spreadsheet from various dates, all of which are vital and must be retained for posterity eternally. If the ARC is using most of the system's memory, it's because a process accessed a file. The ARC doesn't go hunting for excuses to suck up RAM.

Zfs-stats

FreeBSD exposes ZFS performance, settings, and metrics through a variety of sysctls in vfs.zfs and kstat.zfs. These values usually mean very little by themselves, but are illuminating when compared to each other. Rather than parsing those values directly, we highly recommend using the `zfs-stats` package to examine the ARC.

Use `zfs-stats -A` to get basic information about the ARC, such as its current size and the size of each queue within the ARC. Here are interesting snippets from a `zfs-stats` report from one of Lucas' systems.

```
# zfs-stats -A
...
ARC Summary: (HEALTHY)
    Memory Throttle Count:    0
...
```

The Memory Throttle Count tells how many times the ARC has been shrunk to return memory to the kernel for use by another process. If the memory throttle count is high, you might consider lowering the limit on the ARC size to ensure there is enough free memory for your other processes. ARC memory throttling does not mean that a system must have more memory, though, merely that it would make use of additional memory.

```
...
ARC Size:                           36.22%  10.89  GiB
  Target Size: (Adaptive)          100.00%  30.07  GiB
  Min Size (Hard Limit):            12.50%   3.76  GiB
  Max Size (High Water):               8:1  30.07  GiB
...
```

This particular ARC is at 36.22% of its maximum size, or 10.89 GB. It's configured for a maximum size is 30.07 GB. The minimum is 3.76 GB.

```
...
ARC Size Breakdown:
  Recently Used Cache Size:     50.00%  15.03   GiB
  Frequently Used Cache Size:   50.00%  15.03   GiB
...
```

The ARC has evenly divided memory allocated for the MRU and MFU caches.

The ARC efficiency report, given by `zfs-stats -E`, is more interesting than the general report. Here are the most interesting snippets of that output from a different server.

```
# zfs-stats -E
...
ARC Efficiency:                    78.40m
 Cache Hit Ratio:       97.76%  76.65m
 Cache Miss Ratio:       2.24%   1.75m
 Actual Hit Ratio:      97.76%  76.65m
```

ZFS dedicates gobs of memory to filesystem caching. The top of this report shows us how much benefit we get out of this. The Cache Hit Ratio says what percent of disk read requests were served from the ARC rather than by going to disk. In this case, 97.76% of all read requests on this machine were served out of memory. The number after the percentage is the raw number of requests. This host served 76.65 million disk requests out of the ARC.

Next, `zfs-stats` shows which cache a cached file came from.

```
CACHE HITS BY CACHE LIST:
 Most Recently Used:             3.35%   2.57m
 Most Frequently Used:          96.65%  74.08m
 Most Recently Used Ghost:       0.04%  28.81k
 Most Frequently Used Ghost:     0.08%  63.26k
```

The MRU cache, which resembles the traditional buffer cache, served 3.35% of all the files served from the ARC. 96.65% of all files came from the MFU cache. There's certainly some overlap between these queues—in the absence of an MFU cache, some of the frequently accessed files would appear in the MRU cache. But it's a nice illustration of why the ARC uses an MFU cache.

Ghosts hold the lists of data that was recently cached, but was discarded due to memory pressure or other limits. Would adding more memory and increasing the ARC size improve our cache hit rates? With 0.04% and 0.08% hits on the ghost lists, adding more memory wouldn't really improve caching. This host's ARC is only 36% full, so items are not being evicted. Those tiny percentages might be tens of thousands of requests, but compared to the millions of requests it's served, that's almost nothing. Additional memory might improve other processes, but not the ARC.

Next we see the type of data pulled from the ARC.

```
CACHE HITS BY DATA TYPE:
 Demand Data:           97.15%  74.46m
 Prefetch Data:          0.00%       0
 Demand Metadata:        2.85%   2.19m
 Prefetch Metadata:     0.00%        0
```

Data is the content of files, while metadata is everything about the files. We discuss prefetching in Chapter 8, but whatever prefetching is, it clearly doesn't come into play here.

On the flip side of the coin, we see which sorts of data weren't cached.

```
CACHE MISSES BY DATA TYPE:
 Demand Data:           31.72%  556.25k
 Prefetch Data:           0.00%        0
 Demand Metadata:       68.28%    1.20m
 Prefetch Metadata:      0.00%       19
```

How many of a system's requests should get served out of the ARC? That depends entirely on the workload. A web server that serves the same data over and over again could expect high cache hit rates. Expect lower cache hit rates on servers where clients access many different files. If your pool has terabytes of data in millions of files, but clients never access the same data file twice, caching files in memory will not boost performance.

Modifying the ARC

The ZFS ARC manages itself in the overwhelming majority of cases. In most cases where the ARC cannot auto-tune itself, performance problems are best solved by adding hardware. Sometimes, though, adjusting ZFS' memory or performance can buy you time until you can receive and install new hardware. On rare occasion, adjusting the ARC is the proper response for a specific application.

You can tweak the ARC by setting upper and lower boundaries on how much memory it can use, as well as controlling what, when, and why the ARC caches data.

Restricting ARC Size

A default FreeBSD install sets aside 1 GB of RAM for the kernel and operating programs, permitting ZFS to absorb the rest in the ARC if that's what the system performance demands. You can change this by reserving a minimum amount of memory for the ARC and/or setting a hard limit on how much memory the ARC can take.

The ARC settings are all given in bytes. Today, we manage memory in gigabytes. To set a value for ZFS, multiply the desired number of gigabytes by 1024^3.

The ARC surrenders memory readily upon request, but freeing memory doesn't happen instantaneously. Releasing memory from the ARC and allocating it to another process unquestionably takes longer than allocating free memory to that same process. On a host with a very large ARC, dumping gigabytes of objects from the cache might take a measurable fraction of a second.

You might decide to limit the amount of memory the ARC can use, freeing system memory for applications. Use the boot-time tunable vfs.zfs.arc_max to set this. By default, FreeBSD sets this to the total memory minus 1 GB. Here we set an upper limit of 20 GB in */boot/loader.conf*.

```
vfs.zfs.arc_max="21474836480"
```

The maximum ARC size is not a hard limit, but rather more of a high-water mark. When the ARC hits this size, ZFS begins hurriedly reducing the cache size. The least important items get added to the ghost queues and dumped. If you're monitoring the ARC size, you might see memory usage wobble around vfs.zfs.arc_max when the system experiences memory pressure.

It's also possible that an application could use the ARC's generosity against it, and squeeze it out of existence. The default minimum size of the ARC is one-eighth of the maximum size. (Strictly speaking, the minimum ARC size is half of the maximum amount of memory usable for metadata in the ARC, which is one quarter of the maximum ARC size.) Use the boot-time tunable vfs.zfs.arc_min to set a minimum ARC size. Like the maximum size, the minimum size is expressed in bytes. Here I set the minimum ARC size to 4 GB in */boot/loader.conf*.

```
vfs.zfs.arc_min="4294967296"
```

Lucas normally sets upper and lower limits on ARC size only when he's gotten sick of explaining how the ARC works to non-technical managers. "Yes, PostgreSQL can use a lot of memory. The ARC uses memory. But the ARC only caches stuff that PostgreSQL calls for, and PostgreSQL must be up and running to do that, so it's not a problem."[18]

---

18 If you must have this conversation again, do try to not add "Aaargh, how did you possibly earn your air today?" It never goes over well.

FreeBSD 10.2 and later can specify how much memory the ARC should try to leave free for the use of other processes, with the sysctl vfs.zfs.arc_free_target. The value is different than the others in this section because it is specified in pages, not bytes. A page is 4096 bytes of memory, so a value of 2 GB would be expressed as 524288 ($2 * 1024^3 / 4096$). When the amount of free memory drops below this value, the kernel memory reaper runs. The reaper performs two functions: it adjusts the size of the ARC to ensure there is enough free memory, and it defragments the KMEM Arena. While ZFS has been rapidly allocating and freeing bits of memory as files move in and out of the ARC, it has littered bits all over the different segments of kernel memory. That memory is not returned to *free* until all allocations in an arena are freed. This manifests itself as the amount of *wired* memory being significantly higher than the size of the ARC plus the expected other wired pages like the networking stack. Unlike the previous tunables, vfs.zfs.arc_free_target can be adjusted on a running system and takes immediate effect.

Metadata and the ARC

Filesystem metadata includes all the stuff about files, except the files themselves: directories, permissions, ownership, size, properties, and more. The ARC caches all of this information exactly as it caches file contents. Accessing a file's contents requires accessing the file's metadata, after all.

By default, the ARC uses up to one-fourth of its maximum size to cache this metadata. While this is almost always sufficient, if a filesystem has a whole bunch of tiny files, you might need to expand this limit. The boot-time tunable vfs.zfs.arc_meta_limit lets you configure a specific limit for metadata that can be either above or below the default. Here we hard-code the ARC's metadata cache to 8 GB in */boot/loader.conf*.

```
vfs.zfs.arc_meta_limit="8589934592"
```

If `zfs-stats -E` shows that you're drawing much more data than metadata out of the ARC, you might consider increasing the metadata limit and see if performance improves. Remember that by default, the minimum size of the ARC is half of the amount that can be used for metadata. Also, cached metadata cannot use more space than the entire ARC.

Datasets and the ARC

Some data has regular access patterns that make the ARC irrelevant—by the time any file is accessed a second time, it would have long since been expired from the MRU and MFU list. This typically only happens when a dataset contains millions of files and when you can easily predict their usage. Telling the ARC to not cache these files frees up memory to cache files that might benefit.

The ZFS property **`primarycache`** defines what parts of a dataset's information should go into the ARC. The default, *all*, means to cache file data and metadata alike.

Setting **`primarycache`** to *metadata* tells the ARC to only cache each file's metadata, not the contents. You might find this useful for directories that contain large numbers of files. Without metadata caching, running ls(1) on a large directory might take several minutes as ZFS reads the disks and assembles the information. Caching only metadata disables ZFS prefetching, which might hurt performance more than metadata-only caching helps.

Setting **`primarycache`** to *none* tells the ARC to not cache anything from this dataset. You can't prefetch without a cache, but if a dataset isn't cached, performance clearly isn't a concern.

For example, one of Lucas' servers has a multi-terabyte dataset with innumerable files created over the last 15 years. On the rare occasions that these files are accessed, they're searched in order. The server doesn't have nearly enough memory to effectively cache the contents of all these files. Telling the ARC to cache metadata on this dataset means that ls(1) and such still work briskly, but we won't uselessly clutter this machine's ARC.

You must unmount and remount a dataset before changes to the `primarycache` property take effect.

```
# zfs set primarycache=metadata cdr/cdr
# zfs unmount cdr/cdr
# zfs mount cdr/cdr
```

The ARC is now free for useful work, such as caching the temporary files created by analyzing these records.

Unmounting a dataset removes all of the cached information about that dataset from both the ARC and the L2ARC.

Level 2 ARC

The ARC constantly prunes itself to keep within its permitted size. Files that have not been referenced in a long time fall off the MRU list. Normally, items dropped off the ARC evaporate—while they're mentioned on the ghost lists, so the MFU queue can recognize them if they come by again, the system relies on the on-disk copy of the file.

The Level 2 ARC, or *L2ARC*, is a secondary read cache. The L2ARC catches items that fall off of the ARC. By using a small, fast, high-endurance disk to cache ARC data you can simultaneously reduce read load on your system's main storage and improve read performance. The `zpool(8)` command calls an L2ARC a *cache device*.

While the L2ARC is written to disk, the data in it does not survive a reboot. While everything is safely there, the indexes to that data are destroyed. Even if those indexes were available, the pools could have been modified on a different machine before rebooting the system. ZFS cannot trust the information on the cache device.

As of early 2016, there's a nearly complete implementation of a persistent L2ARC. With a persistent L2ARC, the system would reload the prior L2ARC and load everything back into memory. While this feature might never reach wide distribution, heavy L2ARC users might check for it in the future.

Using an L2ARC makes sense when you have multiple users, virtual machines, or applications accessing a single data set. If your working set is larger than the amount of RAM you can afford, your second choice is L2ARC based on SSD or NVMe devices. For most applications, such as the typical home or enterprise NAS, an L2ARC will not increase performance. An L2ARC can even hurt performance through memory consumption.

L2ARC Memory Use

While the L2ARC contains a whole bunch of cached data and metadata, the index to that data resides within the ARC. As a general rule of thumb, each gigabyte of L2ARC requires about 25 MB of ARC. (This varies with the sector size of the disk, the `recordsize` property, and other dataset characteristics, which makes the actual size notoriously difficult to calculate.) It's fairly sane to assume that one terabyte of L2ARC, fully utilized, will devour about 25 GB of ARC.

Most L2ARCs are not nearly a terabyte—at least, not yet. SSDs of sufficiently high endurance to make them suitable for read caches are still expensive enough that most of us don't have them lying around. Those of you planning massive storage arrays with more than, say, 40 drives, should remember this.

L2ARC Caching

The L2ARC can only cache data that falls off the ARC. Data that is never in the ARC cannot appear in the L2ARC.

Suppose you've completely disabled ARC caching for all datasets on a particular pool by setting the `primarycache` property to *none*. Adding an L2ARC to this pool will not improve ZFS performance. There is no cached data to fall down to the L2ARC.

You might think it makes sense to have a dataset where the ARC contains the metadata, while the L2ARC caches the actual file data. Lucas' multi-terabyte *cdr/cdr* dataset from the previous section might seem a great candidate for this. And once he sets `primarycache` to *metadata*, it sure looks like that's what will happen.

```
# zfs get primarycache,secondarycache zroot/cdr
NAME        PROPERTY        VALUE     SOURCE
zroot/cdr   primarycache    metadata  local
zroot/cdr   secondarycache  all       default
```

The problem is that the ARC only caches metadata, so the only stuff it can push to the L2ARC is metadata. The L2ARC can contain only what's in the ARC, or a subset thereof.

By default the ARC caches everything the system accesses, so the L2ARC does the same.

You can control how each dataset uses the L2ARC with the `secondarycache` property. As with the `primarycache` property, `secondarycache` can be set to *all*, *metadata*, or *none*. The default is *all*, meaning that data that's almost important enough for the primary ARC gets pushed off onto the L2ARC.

Streaming Files

Most of the time needed to read a file is spent moving the disk heads into position over the platter. Once positioned, the heads read data pretty quickly. This is called *streaming*. While serving large files out of memory would be faster than reading them from disk, on most systems the multiple disks of the main pool are faster than the one or two disks of the L2ARC. In this case, having the L2ARC cache streaming files doesn't make sense, so it's disabled by default.

If you have an L2ARC that's faster than your main pool, you might want to enable large file caching. The boot-time tunable vfs.zfs.l2arc_noprefetch controls caching of streaming files. The default setting, *1*, disables caching streaming files. Set this to *0* to enable caching, as in this example from */boot/loader.conf*.

```
vfs.zfs.l2arc_noprefetch=0
```

This tunable only takes effect when importing the pool. FreeBSD imports pools before looking at */etc/sysctl.conf*, so this must be set in the boot loader.

L2ARC Write Speed

SSDs are not as robust as spinning disks. Even if you contact a specialist vendor (such as iX Systems) who's very familiar with ZFS and knows precisely the best disk to use for an L2ARC, you can hammer on an SSD only so much before it dies. While ZFS gracefully manages a dying or dead L2ARC, constant disk death is expensive, time consuming, and annoying to the sysadmin. ZFS implements a couple of write throttles on the L2ARC to extend disk life.

Like the main ARC, the L2ARC uses bytes in its configuration. Most L2ARC settings make the most sense in megabytes. Multiply your desired values by 1024^2.

During normal operating, ZFS only writes 8 MB per second to each L2ARC device. This avoids wearing out the SSD device, and also helps avoid cache thrashing. (*Cache thrashing* is writing a lot of data to the cache that just ends up getting overwritten with newer data before it's used.) If you need a system's L2ARC to handle more data, you can boost this with the sysctl vfs.zfs.l2arc_write_max. Don't turn this up so high that you make reads slow.

When a system first boots, the L2ARC is empty. An empty L2ARC doesn't do much good. ZFS does a Turbo Warmup Phase after system boot where it writes extra data to the L2ARC, over and above the limit set by vfs.zfs.l2arc_write_max. Turbo Warmup Phase continues until the ARC drops the first item from the L2ARC. The length of time this takes depends entirely on the system. By default, ZFS can write an extra 8 MB to each L2ARC device during Turbo Warmup Phase. The sysctl vfs.zfs.l2arc_write_boost controls the extra bandwidth allocated.

You can change these sysctls at any time. Here we set both to 16 MB.

```
# sysctl vfs.zfs.l2arc_write_max=16777216
vfs.zfs.l2arc_write_max: 8388608 -> 16777216
# sysctl vfs.zfs.l2arc_write_boost=16777216
vfs.zfs.l2arc_write_boost: 8388608 -> 16777216
```

Software settings will not let you exceed the hardware's limitations, of course.

SSDs are not as notoriously fragile as they once were. A modern data center class SSD, like a 200 GB Intel DC S3700, has an Endurance Rating of "10 drive writes per day for 5 years." This translates to around 2,000 GB per day, or 23 MB/second. You could constantly write 23 MB/s to this drive, and according to Intel it would endure for five years. On a high-performance server, tuning the throttle sysctls up to these values and adding a note to order a new cache device in 58 months would make sense. As your host probably won't write to the L2ARC at full throttle all of the time, turning these parameters even higher might make sense.

ZFS Intent Log

Caches aren't just for reading data. ZFS uses caches for writes as well, through the ZFS Intent Log (ZIL). ZFS dumps writes to the ZIL, and then processes those writes to add them properly to ZFS. Every pool has its own ZIL. In normal use, ZFS uses a chunk of space on each provider for the ZIL. If you desire, you can add an external device for use as a ZIL. Strictly speaking, the ZIL isn't exactly a write cache. But it's sort of cachey, so we'll cover it in this chapter.

The ZIL doesn't work the way most people think it does, however. To understand when a pool needs a separate logging device and when it doesn't, you must understand how ZFS writes data.

Sync and Async Transactions

ZFS is all about the integrity of data that reaches permanent storage. Data on the disk should always be coherent. A system might lose data in between the program and the disk, but no filesystem can protect in-flight data residing only in RAM.

To ensure on-disk data integrity, ZFS groups write requests in transaction groups, or *txgs*. A transaction group is a bunch of data and the associated filesystem metadata. When you ask the system to write to disk, ZFS collects those writes in a transaction group. One transaction group can include writes from many unrelated processes. Once the group has enough data or a timer expires, that transaction group gets written to the disk. That timer might be as long as 30 seconds or as short as five, depending on which release of FreeBSD you're running.

A transaction group is the filesystem's to-do list. Exactly like your to-do list, if something horrible happens the list gets thrown to the wolves[19]. Data is vulnerable to system failure until it is completely written to the disk. If the system crashes or dies before the transaction group is written to disk, that data is lost. Reducing the transaction group timeout might reduce the amount of data loss, but it also badly impacts performance.

---

19 Wolves, of course, don't care about paper lists. For this metaphor to work well, we suggest writing your to-do lists on rump roasts.

As the sysadmin, it's your job to manage the risk of data loss. Let's walk through writing data to disk.

A program hands the kernel a chunk of data and says, "Please write this to the disk." The program does not proceed until the kernel acknowledges receipt of the data. Once the kernel says, "I have the data," the program continues. A program waiting for this response is said to be *blocking on I/O.*

The important question is: when does the kernel acknowledge receipt of the data? When the data is added to a transaction group, or when it's written to disk?

In normal operation, the kernel acknowledges the data when the data is in memory as part of a pending transaction group. The data is not on the disk—the kernel has merely claimed responsibility for the data. If the system were a restaurant, dinner would now be in the waiter's hands on the way to the customer, but the waiter could still trip. Variants on asynchronous operation are common among modern filesystems, such as the various versions of Linux's extfs and BSD UFS.

A filesystem can also work in synchronous mode, where the kernel acknowledges data only when the bits are actually written to the physical storage medium. Sync mounts are extremely safe, but also extremely slow. The program that wrote the data will block waiting for the physical hardware to respond to the kernel's write request. Certain programs, such as database servers, request synchronous acknowledgement for particular files by using the fsync(2) system call. The sysadmin might mount the dataset synchronously, so that the system only acknowledges data when the write is complete, or could use the fsync(8) program to tell the system to flush everything to disk right now.

ZFS Intent Log

When ZFS writes files in synchronous mode, it doesn't immediately push a transaction group to the disk. Instead, those writes get dumped on the ZIL. They're not neatly ordered as ZFS dataset blocks; instead, they're just a heap of blocks on the disk. When the transaction group gets written to disk, the blocks on the ZIL get written to their proper location.

The pool import process checks the ZIL for data that hasn't yet reached its final home. If the system finds in-flight blocks in a pool it's importing, it completes those transactions.

Pools normally use a small chunk of space on each storage provider as the ZIL. Yes, this means each synchronous write gets written to physical storage twice. But the pool only uses the ZIL for synchronously-written data. Normal, asynchronous writes get stored in RAM and committed as part of a regular transaction group.

You can sometimes improve performance by putting the ZIL on a dedicated, fast device, called a Separate Intent LOG.

Separate Intent Log

You can separate the ZIL from the pool by using a Separate Intent Log, or *SLOG*. By moving the ZIL to separate, dedicated hardware, you avoid writing the same data twice to the storage providers. If the SLOG hardware is faster than the pool, the kernel can acknowledge the data more quickly, improving the performance of the requesting application.

Despite common usage, a SLOG is not the same thing as a ZIL. The SLOG is the hardware. A ZIL lives on either the SLOG or the storage providers. You can launch the SLOG through a window, but you can only swear at the ZIL.

The fastest, most reliable, and most expensive SLOG is an NVRAM chip. High-endurance SSDs are the most common choice for SLOG. You can even use very fast SAS drives, but they're the least reliable. Every one of these needs a private power source, such as a battery or a supercapacitor, to let them complete writes in case of a system power failure.

A SLOG does not need to be large. The sysctl vfs.zfs.dirty_data_max gives the maximum possible amount of in-flight data. FreeBSD 10's ZFS defaults to using a ZIL with a size equal to one-tenth of the system RAM. You could use a single piece of hardware to support SLOG providers for more than one pool, but that also splits that device's I/O between those pools. One reason for using a SLOG is to cope with I/O shortages.

Not all SSDs or NVRAMs are created equal. Many devices marketed as "high endurance" aren't robust enough to handle all the writes for even a medium-sized pool. For an application where data integrity is vital, the authors strongly encourage you to consult with a hardware vendor that specializes in ZFS, such as iX Systems (http://www.ixsystems.com). A properly chosen SLOG can vastly accelerate your programs, while a poor choice can corrupt your pool.

Per-Dataset ZIL Tuning

You can control how (or if) a dataset uses the ZIL with the `sync` property. Much like mounting a traditional filesystem sync or async, the `sync` property dictates whether the dataset honors fsync(2) requests.

The default setting, *standard*, tells the dataset to use the ZIL for synchronous requests. If a program uses fsync(2) to request that the kernel not acknowledge the data until it's safely on disk, the data gets written to the ZIL. Other data is written asynchronously, as part of a transaction group. This is the default.

Setting **sync** to *always* sends all writes to the ZIL. No writes are asynchronous. This is the safest way to manage data, but it has a serious performance penalty. You might choose to set this property on datasets dedicated to critical data.

Setting **sync** to *disabled* completely disables use of the ZIL on this dataset. All writes are asynchronous. The system lies to every program that uses sync(2). Never, never disable the ZIL on any dataset used by a database or NFS. Really, the only reason to disable the ZIL on a dataset is to verify that the ZIL is not causing your particular application a performance problem. If disabling the ZIL fixes your application, definitely file a bug report or install a fast SLOG device.

In almost all cases, leave **sync** at *standard*. You might have one or two datasets that need `sync` to be set at *always*.

Synchronous Writes through the Stack

ZFS winds up as the data storage backend for many different applications, such as the Network File System (NFS) and iSCSI. You might use a zvol for a virtualized system's drive. All of these different layers operate independently. While they can talk to each other through the common system calls and APIs, they don't control each other. Each layer of an application stack can (and routinely does) lie to the other layers. And nowhere is this more obvious, and more dangerous, than the fsync(2) system call.

Suppose you have a virtual machine that runs off an iSCSI drive, backed by a zvol on your server. The virtual machine's operating system requests a synchronous disk write. The iSCSI stack takes that request and passes it to ZFS. If you set **sync** to *disabled* on that zvol ZFS sniggers, says "Synchronous? Sure! You got it, buddy," and waits to do anything until the next txg.

You might set **sync** to *always* on the zvol, accepting the performance hit in the name of data integrity. But if the iSCSI stack disables synchronous writes, you'll take that hit without any benefit. Any layer of a complex application stack might disable synchronous writes.

If data integrity is important, verify that synchronous writes work throughout your application stack.

zpool.cache

Now let's discuss a cache that you'll hear about, but that doesn't affect day-to-day system administration: the file */boot/zfs/zpool.cache*.

The *zpool.cache* file contains a description of the pools currently active on the system and their providers. When you boot a ZFS system, the kernel checks the *zpool.cache* file on the root pool to discover which of the system's pools it should import.

ZFS' zdb(8) uses information in the cache file for debugging. You can't use the debugger on a pool without a cache.

You can control the cache file's location with the **cachefile** property. Here, we change the cache file for the pool *work*.

```
# zpool set cachefile=/work/zfs/work.zpool.cache work
```

Despite much lingering, obsolete documentation to the contrary, there's almost never a reason to change the cachefile location on modern versions of ZFS or FreeBSD.

Now that you understand the cache, we can talk about performance.

Chapter 8: Performance

We all like our storage to be fast, featureful, and infinite. We haven't quite hit infinite capacity yet, but on good hardware ZFS' features can be pretty fast. Even the best hardware can turn slow for no apparent reason, however. Knowing how to use the diagnostic tools can help you understand a system's performance. Maybe you can't fix it with the equipment on hand, but at least you'll understand what's going wrong and maybe shift some of the load elsewhere.

FreeBSD includes tools to check both generic disk and filesystem performance as well as ZFS-specific tools. You can get detailed information through sysctl(8), vmstat(8), and related commands, but we strongly recommend installing the add-on package `zfs-stats` to conveniently parse and process that information.

Once you understand how to assess system performance, we'll discuss several ZFS performance features and when they might be useful.

Before diving into assessing ZFS performance, let's talk a bit about performance in general.

What Is Performance?

Performance might be described as "how well a system manages a workload." Every system has a slightly different workload, so performance varies even between identical hardware performing seemingly identical tasks. Even if you try very hard to replicate hardware, software installations, and workload on another system, somebody can find a difference between them. That's part of what makes benchmarking so annoying.

A system administrator mostly cares about improving performance. This means identifying and removing bottlenecks. The average computer has four basic resources: storage input/output, network bandwidth, memory, and CPU. If you pile work on a system until it can't handle any more, what you're really doing is discovering which of these four resources you saturate first. That resource is your bottleneck.

Increasing performance requires identifying and shifting bottlenecks. And you'll always hit another bottleneck. If your CPU is the current bottleneck, and you add more processing power, the computer speeds up until it saturates disk I/O or memory or the network. You've improved performance, yes … up to the limit permitted by the new bottleneck.

And a different workload probably has a completely different bottleneck.

A lot of systems administration requires exchanging one of these four resources for another. It's why Lucas always refers to "system tuning" as "rearranging bottlenecks."[20]

Consider ZFS compression for a moment. ZFS compression reduces the amount of data the system writes to, and pulls from, the disk. Compressing and decompressing blocks consumes processor time. Compression exchanges storage I/O for CPU time. Most computers have far more processor oomph than they can possibly use, however. The laptop I'm writing this on has a four-core processor, but a single middling-speed disk with very limited I/O. Enabling compression is an obvious win on this system. On a system with more disk I/O than processor power, you might make a different decision.

---

20 Lucas calls many things "rearranging bottlenecks." He solves the "dirty clothing" bottleneck by expending the time and detergent resources. At the precise moment you're reading this, he's almost certainly suffering from a gelato bottleneck.

The more complicated your storage is, the more you can adjust and shift storage bottlenecks. Your server has six disk controllers, but all the I/O is going to one of them? Rearrange your datasets to split the load across multiple controllers. Maybe a particular disk is saturated? Split up that load. Perhaps your pools are saturated with writes, or reads, or both. Add a properly configured SLOG and an L2ARC to help.

Before you make any changes, though, investigate where the bottleneck is. Purchasing a faster disk system won't help if your system's particular workload is limited by CPU or memory. Adding a fast SSD for a ZIL won't improve performance if disk reads throttle the server's performance.

One of many perennial questions in systems administration is: what's eating up my disk bandwidth? A ZFS pool scrub can impact other operations, but in routine use, ZFS doesn't create any new answers to this question. Use `top -m io` to identify the processes using the disk most intensively. Should the most active processes be that busy?

If your performance doesn't match your expectations, remember that your storage system performs only as well as its slowest component. You can have a really fast SAS controller and top-of-the-line, high-speed hard drives but get terrible performance because of the cruddy drive cables. A SATA port multiplier slashes performance proportionally to the number of drives attached. Just because you can plug certain hardware components together, doesn't mean you should.

ZFS and Performance

Much of the usual storage performance tuning advice applies to ZFS as it does any other filesystem. If you don't need to know when a file was last used, disable recording access time with the `atime` property.

ZFS is designed to work with lots of disk space. A pool that's more than 80 percent full performs badly. That's inherent in how ZFS is put together. If you're trying to figure out why an almost full pool is running slowly, move some of the data to another pool. Releasing space on a nearly full pool alleviates most ZFS issues.

ZFS is also designed to work with 64-bit systems. With some persuasion, luck, and a little traditional Haitian voodoo, you can get ZFS to work on 32-bit FreeBSD. It won't work well, and it won't be efficient—but the system will boot. Becoming frustrated with ZFS performance on 32-bit systems is like getting annoyed at the dancing bear with a poor sense of rhythm. In both cases, the amazing thing is that it works at all.

If the usual sysadmin advice for increasing filesystem performance doesn't help solve your problems, you must dive in and see why your storage system is behaving poorly. Every operating system includes tools for measuring performance. FreeBSD's vmstat(8) can quickly identify if your system is waiting for processor, storage, or memory.

To see how well your pools perform, use `zpool iostat`.

zpool iostat

The `iostat` component of `zpool` gives a snapshot of how your pools are performing at a particular instant in time. To see average activity on your pools since the system booted, run `zpool iostat`.

```
# zpool iostat
           capacity     operations  bandwidth
pool    alloc   free   read  write   read  write
-----   -----  -----  -----  -----  -----  -----
work    2.21G  1.81T      2    402  36.2K  24.0M
zroot   15.5G   905G    275      0  7.34M      0
```

We have the name of each pool, with the amount of allocated and free space in each. The last four columns display each pool's read and write activity, in units of both operations per second and bytes per second.

This example shows two pools, *work* and *zroot*. The *zroot* pool has 15.5 GB allocated and 905 GB free. The pool is doing 275 read operations per second, or 7.34 MB per second, and no write operations. This means each read operation averages around 27 KB (7.34 MB / 275 = 27 KB).

The *work* pool is more interesting. We have two read requests per second, but 402 writes per second for a total of 24 MB/s. The reads are negligible, but each write averages about 60 KB. There's actual work happening here.

What does this mean for your pool? Taken on its own, not much. This is the pool activity at a particular instant. This instant might be average, or it might be a high or low period. You need an ongoing view of pool activity to make any sensible decisions.

To view the activity for a single pool, give the pool a name.

```
# zpool iostat work
```

This eliminates all output except that for the specified pool.

Remember, this is an average of behavior since the system booted. It doesn't reflect current values.

Current & Ongoing Pool Activity

To see how the pool is behaving at this particular moment, and how activity changes over time, have `zpool iostat` print new statistics every few seconds. Specify a number of seconds at the end of the command line. Here we get updates every two seconds. Hit CTRL-C to exit.

```
# zpool iostat 2
               capacity     operations     bandwidth
pool        alloc   free   read  write   read  write
-----       -----  -----  -----  -----  -----  -----
work        3.37G  1.81T     14    107   146K   900K
zroot       15.5G   905G      3      2  32.9K  12.7K
-----       -----  -----  -----  -----  -----  -----
work        3.37G  1.81T      0      0      0      0
zroot       15.5G   905G      0      0      0      0
-----       -----  -----  -----  -----  -----  -----
```

The first entry is the average activity since the system booted, exactly as if you had run `zpool iostat` without an interval. The second and later entries give current values.

After the headers, the first two entries give the pool activity when you first run the command and a set of dotted lines. Two seconds later, it prints a new set of data below the separator.

If you specify checking a single pool, `zpool iostat` loses the separators. Here we look at the *work* pool.

```
# zpool iostat work 2
               capacity     operations     bandwidth
pool        alloc   free   read  write   read  write
-----       -----  -----  -----  -----  -----  -----
work        3.35G  1.81T     15    104   148K   897K
work        3.35G  1.81T      0    616  2.25K  3.74M
work        3.35G  1.81T      1    553  5.74K  2.78M
work        3.36G  1.81T      1    607  21.0K  2.57M
...
```

This pool averages 104 write operations per second, but at this moment it's doing over 600 write operations per second. It's doing real work!

Virtual Device Activity

While each pool contains one or more identical virtual devices, the pool's usage of those virtual devices might not be identical.

One common situation is when you have a nearly full pool and add a new virtual device to it to gain more space. The pool's apparent write performance might then drop to that of the new virtual device, rather than the theoretical throughput of the entire pool with all its virtual devices. The new virtual device has all of the free space, so that's where the new writes go. Over time, as you delete old files and remove old snapshots, per-VDEV utilization might average out. Depending on your workload, however, VDEV utilization might never reach equilibrium.

To view per-VDEV activity of each pool, add the `-v` flag after `iostat`.

Like regular non-verbose `zpool iostat`, the first set of output you get represents the average since the system booted. In verbose mode, these numbers look kind of weird.

```
# zpool iostat -v work
               capacity     operations    bandwidth
pool         alloc   free   read  write   read  write
----------   -----  -----  -----  -----  -----  -----
work         2.13G  1.81T     10     87   100K   715K
  mirror     1.06G   927G      5     43  50.9K   359K
    gpt/zfs0     -      -      2      8  26.4K   360K
    gpt/zfs1     -      -      2      8  26.6K   360K
  mirror     1.07G   927G      4     43  49.6K   356K
    gpt/zfs2     -      -      2      8  25.0K   357K
    gpt/zfs3     -      -      2      8  26.4K   357K
----------   -----  -----  -----  -----  -----  -----
```

You'll get a total for the pool, totals for each VDEV in the pool, and a number for each provider in the pool. Look at the write operations per second on this pool. The pool as a whole has averaged 10 read operations per second since system boot. The first mirror device is responsible for five of these, the second for four of them. Each disk within each virtual device handles two reads per second.[21]

---

21 These are averages, so don't let the fact that ZFS thinks 2+2=5 worry you. ZFS' checksum functionality does math more properly.

The write activity looks downright strange. ZFS' initial data shows that this pool averages 87 write requests per second, with 43 coming from each pool. That's not bad—but the per-disk values show that each disk averages eight write requests a second. No matter how grotesquely you round these values, they aren't even close.

The short answer is, ZFS' per-disk averages are not very reliable as raw numbers. They're proportionally correct. The `zpool iostat` doesn't lock in-kernel data structures while measuring performance, so you'll get slight variations as the command runs.

Just as with non-verbose `zpool iostat`, to see current values you must provide an interval at the end of your command line. Here we show the per-device activity on the pool work, updating every two seconds.

```
# zpool iostat -v work 2
...
               capacity     operations     bandwidth
pool         alloc   free   read  write   read  write
----------   -----  -----  -----  -----  -----  -----
work         2.31G  1.81T      0     69      0   147K
  mirror     1.15G   927G      0     40      0  93.6K
    gpt/zfs0     -      -      0     10      0  94.9K
    gpt/zfs1     -      -      0     10      0  94.9K
  mirror     1.16G   927G      0     28      0  53.3K
    gpt/zfs2     -      -      0      6      0  54.6K
    gpt/zfs3     -      -      0      6      0  54.6K
----------   -----  -----  -----  -----  -----  -----
```

The first mirror VDEV performs more I/O operations per second than the second mirror. Again, the individual disk numbers don't add up to the total number of operations in the device, but they're proportionally accurate.

Now that you can see how well your pools are working, let's discuss some features that can change how well your pool performs.

ZFS Prefetch

The job of a filesystem is to provide stored data on request. ZFS takes that idea further, by getting ready to provide data you're about to ask for. This takes place on two levels, per-VDEV and per-file. FreeBSD doesn't enable per-VDEV prefetch by default, but enables per-file prefetching.

Per-VDEV Prefetch

The most time-consuming part of retrieving data from a spinning disk is positioning the heads over the tracks containing the data. It's like making a sandwich—slapping peanut butter between two slices of bread takes two minutes, but going to the store to get bread and peanut butter might take you an hour. Once the hardware is physically arranged, reading a full track of data off of a disk spinning at 5,000 or 10,000 RPM takes microseconds.

Per-VDEV prefetch is an attempt to make moving the heads worthwhile. FreeBSD does not use per-VDEV prefetching by default, but if your workload involves complicated metadata, complex or large directory trees, or many small files, per-VDEV prefetch might help you.

Whenever ZFS reads a few blocks off the VDEV, it also reads the few blocks after the target blocks, looking for metadata. Any metadata found gets stuffed into a special per-VDEV prefetch cache. There's a good chance that the requesting program will return and ask for that metadata. Each time a program requests that prefetched metadata, ZFS provides it from the cache, returns to the physical VDEV, and prefetches more blocks.

Per-VDEV prefetched blocks go into a simple rolling Least Recently Used cache, not the ARC. If the blocks are never called, they quickly get discarded. The size of a VDEV's cache equals the number of storage providers in the VDEV times the tunable vfs.zfs.vdev.cache.size. FreeBSD sets this to *0* by default, so the cache is not used. Enable the cache by setting this tunable to the desired value in `/boot/loader.conf`. A common value is 10 MB.

```
vfs.zfs.vdev.cache.size="10M"
```

After a reboot, you'll have a per-VDEV prefetch cache in play.

The sysctl kstat.zfs.misc.vdev_cache_stats.misses shows how many times ZFS checked the per-VDEV cache for metadata and didn't find it. Similarly, the sysctl kstat.zfs.misc.vdev_cache_stats.hits shows how often ZFS found something in the cache.

Test your workload with and without per-VDEV prefetch and see how it behaves.

How much does per-VDEV prefetching preemptively cache? The sysctl vfs.zfs.vdev.cache.max gives the minimal size of a read from a VDEV. This defaults to 16384, or 16 KB. If a program requests a read smaller than this size, per-VDEV prefetching kicks in.

The read isn't just expanded to 16 KB, however. The sysctl vfs.zfs.vdev.cache.bshift gives the amount of data to be prefetched and searched for metadata. This is a bit shift value, so the default of 16 means 64 KB.

So, if a program requests a read smaller than 16 KB, ZFS reads 64 KB instead. If a program requests a read of, say, 20 KB, no per-VDEV prefetching occurs.

While changing the prefetch values helped performance with some older versions of ZFS, in modern ZFS you should almost always leave them alone. The authors are not aware of any situations in which changing these values helps, but we do know of many times when changing these values causes suffering.

Per-File Prefetch

If a program requests the start of a file, it'll probably want the rest of the file before long. ZFS' per-file prefetching tries to anticipate such requests, caching the file in the ARC before the program gets around to asking for it. This makes ZFS feel more responsive. This is often called ZFS' *intelligent prefetch*, or sometimes just *prefetch*. While file-level prefetching might not appear terribly sophisticated, most filesystems don't manage it.

File-level prefetch increases the size of the ARC. FreeBSD automatically disables prefetching on hosts with less than 4 GB of RAM, and automatically enables it for hosts with 4 GB or more. You can override this by setting the tunable vfs.zfs.prefetch_disable to *1* in */boot/loader.conf*.

Prefetch can cause problems on systems that host hundreds of thousands (or more) tiny files, such as 64 KB and smaller. You'll want to disable file-level prefetch for such hosts. Those systems are fairly rare, however.

Normally, file-level prefetch improves performance if your system has sufficient memory to support it. You can enable and disable prefetch to test performance, but in almost all cases prefetch is helpful.

Transaction Group Tuning

You can tune performance by adjusting transaction groups and the I/O scheduler. We're specifically covering tuning FreeBSD 10 and later. The mechanisms for tuning OpenZFS writes in earlier versions were considerably more baroque.

A transaction group, or *txg*, is a single lump of data written to disk in an ordered manner. A transaction group can contain many blocks from many different programs. If the entire transaction group is not successfully written to the disk, the entire group is canceled.

You can control how often the system writes a transaction group and its maximum size.

txg Timing

If nothing else triggers writing a txg to disk, ZFS write every few seconds, as given by the sysctl vfs.zfs.txg.timeout. While the value of this setting flailed around a bit in earlier releases of OpenZFS, the current standard is five seconds. Worst case, any pending data gets written to disk every five seconds.

For most systems, writing every five seconds is fine. A program like top(1) might show a burst of CPU activity every five seconds as the pending transaction group gets compressed. You rarely would reduce the timeout to less than five seconds.

Increasing the value might make sense for some systems, however. If you're running ZFS on a low-load virtual machine, you might crank the txg timeout up to 15 or so. Lucas often runs hosts like LDAP mirrors and authoritative DNS servers on virtual machines, and these kinds of hosts rarely have high demand for disk I/O. Reducing the frequency of transaction writes wouldn't improve performance on this particular virtual machine, but it would improve hardware access for other VMs running on that hypervisor. Giving all the virtual machines on that host similarly low settings would improve performance for virtual machines across the board, but a single selfish or high-load VM could eat up many of those gains. (That might be exactly what you're trying to achieve, however.)

On typical hardware that shares reading and writing bandwidth, increasing the timeout might improve read performance most of the time, but will degrade read performance during writes.

If the timer expires and the system has no transactions waiting to be written to disk, ZFS won't write any data. ZFS won't write an empty transaction just for the sake of having a transaction group. It still increments the transaction group count, however.

Setting the transaction group timeout to less than five seconds runs up against the I/O scheduler and the write throttle. For most of us, five seconds is the minimum sensible value.

txg Size

A txg that grows sufficiently large gets committed to disk before the timeout. FreeBSD auto-tunes the maximum size of a transaction group at boot time based on the amount of memory in the host and the tunable vfs.zfs.dirty_data_max_percent. The default is 10,[22] up to a maximum of 4 GB, and is controlled by vfs.zfs.dirty_data_max_max. Once a transaction group uses 10 percent of a system's RAM, it gets written to disk.

You can change the maximum size of a transaction group after boot with the sysctl vfs.zfs.dirty_data_max. This value is in bytes, so multiply your desired number of gigabytes by 1024^3 to get the proper sysctl value.

The hard question is: *should* you change the size of the transaction group? How long does it take your system to write 10 percent of RAM to disk, and how often does that happen? Most hosts have far more RAM than they have I/O throughput. Trying to write one tenth of RAM to disk in five seconds would be a disaster. Lucas' test host has several hard drives in a single pool and 32 GB of RAM. Writing 3.2 GB to disk takes over 20 seconds. If this host generated 3.2 GB of disk activity in less than the standard five-second txg timeout, the machine would quickly spiral into unusability.

---

22 You can change vfs.zfs.dirty_data_max_percent after boot. It won't affect system performance in any way, but you can change it.

If your system has a high-performance disk array with great big gobs of throughput and an economy-sized pile of RAM, though, you might find increasing the maximum value useful.

During these "write cycles," most reading from disk is suspended. This allows the write to complete as quickly as possible. Reading resumes once writing is complete. "Interleaving" the workload like this usually increases performance. Using knowledge of your workload, you can decide if flushing larger transaction groups less often or smaller ones more often is the best approach. When bulk copying data inside the same pool, Jude increased the txg size to 24 GB and the timeout to 30 seconds, and improved performance by 25 percent.

txg Duration and Contents

If you're trying to tune the size and period of transaction groups, it makes sense to ask how large your transaction groups are and how long they take to commit to disk. Adam Leventhal has created some DTrace scripts useful for measuring both, available at http://dtrace.org/blogs/ahl/2014/08/31/openzfs-tuning/ or at http://zfsbook.com. We'll discuss both.

To measure the amount of data in each txg, use Leventhal's script *dirty.d*. ("Dirty data" is in memory, waiting to be written to disk.)

```
txg-syncing
{
  this->dp = (dsl_pool_t *)arg0;
}

txg-syncing
/this->dp->dp_spa->spa_name == $$1/
{
 printf("%4dMB of %4dMB used", this->dp->dp_dirty_total / 1024 / 1024,
   `zfs_dirty_data_max / 1024 / 1024);
}
```

Run this script giving the name of a pool as an argument.

```
# dtrace -s dirty.d zroot
dtrace: script 'dirty.d' matched 2 probes
CPU     ID   FUNCTION:NAME
  3  61042    :txg-syncing  2MB of 6539MB used
  1  61042    :txg-syncing  7MB of 6539MB used
  4  61042    :txg-syncing  5MB of 6539MB used
...
```

DTrace prints the size of each txg, and the size of the ARC, every time ZFS writes the txg to disk. If you change the interval between transaction groups with the vfs.zfs.txg.timeout sysctl, you'll see the sizes of the transaction groups change.

Leventhal's *duration.d* shows how long each transaction group takes to complete.

```
txg-syncing
/((dsl_pool_t *)arg0)->dp_spa->spa_name == $$1/
{
 start = timestamp;
}

txg-synced
/start && ((dsl_pool_t *)arg0)->dp_spa->spa_name == $$1/
{
 this->d = timestamp - start;
 printf("sync took %d.%02d seconds", this->d / 1000000000,
  this->d / 10000000 % 100);
}
```

Use it exactly like the first script, giving the pool name as an argument.

```
# dtrace -s duration.d zroot
dtrace: script 'duration.d' matched 2 probes
CPU     ID   FUNCTION:NAME
  1  61043      :txg-synced sync took 0.11 seconds
  2  61043      :txg-synced sync took 0.24 seconds
  4  61043      :txg-synced sync took 0.22 seconds
  2  61043      :txg-synced sync took 0.31 seconds
```

Despite our best efforts, ZFS isn't working very hard on this system.

If you see that your transaction groups are bouncing up against the maximum txg size, you might want to either increase the txg size or decrease the time between transaction groups.

Once you get the hang of these, Jude created a script that measures both of these simultaneously.

```
#!/usr/sbin/dtrace -s
txg-syncing
/((dsl_pool_t *)arg0)>dp_spa>spa_name == $$1/
{
 start = timestamp;
 this->dp = (dsl_pool_t *)arg0;
 d_total = this->dp->dp_dirty_total;
 d_max = `zfs_dirty_data_max`;
}
txg-synced
/start && ((dsl_pool_t *)arg0)>dp_spa>spa_name == $$1/
{
 this->d = timestamp - start;
 printf("%4dMB of %4dMB synced in %d.%02d seconds",
 d_total / 1024 / 1024,
 d_max / 1024 / 1024, this->d / 1000000000,
 this->d / 10000000 % 100);
}
```

Simultaneously viewing txg size and timing can provide additional insight into how your pool really behaves.

Write Throttle

One term you'll hear thrown about is the *write throttle*. The write throttle comes into play when a program feeds data into memory faster than ZFS can write it to disk. As the system RAM gets more and more full, ZFS starts inserting a small delay into each write request. Programs wait until they get a response to their write requests, so putting a delay here forces them to slow down. The goal is to determine how much load the disks can take, and slow down programs so that they run at exactly that speed.

In older versions of ZFS, the write throttle caused very irregular performance. The write throttle algorithm in FreeBSD 10 and newer works much more smoothly. You can tune it through the I/O scheduler, discussed next.

I/O Scheduling

Not all hardware is created equal. Jude's top-of-the-line laptop has a lot less I/O capacity than any of his Content Delivery Network servers. FreeBSD's default settings are fairly generic. While you don't really need to tune them on a laptop, if you have dozens or hundreds of disks with very specific workloads you can adjust performance through tuning the scheduling. Scheduling I/O lets you adjust latency and throughput.

Throughput is the amount of data that can be read from and written to the storage device. When you say that SATA-3 can transfer data at 6.0 GB/s, you're talking about throughput.

Latency is the length of time the system needs to service those requests. A complicated storage system, with Fiber Channel busses and multiple shelves in multiple parts of the building, might induce latency as requests traverse the system. Your laptop is more likely to have storage latency when you overload the hard drive by copying too many files simultaneously.

While hard drives are generally marketed with a description of how many I/O operations they can perform per second (IOPS), that isn't as useful a term as you might think. Being able to perform 250 IOPS of carefully selected data says nothing about the drive's ability to perform with *your* data.

Think of hard drives like automobiles. Some are optimized for capacity, others for mileage. A huge tandem tractor-trailer rig can haul far more stuff than a Tesla Roadster, but it sure isn't snappy off the red light. Most of us would use the big truck to move a hundred-person call center across town over the weekend, but prefer different optimizations to get a child to the hospital before her appendix finished rupturing.

Unlike a car, you can to a certain extent control the optimization of most hard drives. (Some specialty storage devices are specifically designed for certain optimizations.) That's why you can dump huge amounts of data on your laptop's hard drive and make the system seem unresponsive—you've just exchanged throughput for latency.

ZFS I/O scheduling is designed to smooth out latency. This can reduce throughput, but makes the overall experience more consistent. Generally, by changing the scheduling, you're trying to improve performance while not introducing too much latency.

ZFS scheduling is built around I/O queues.

Measuring Latency and Throughput

How do you know if a change positively affects system performance? You measure it. Adam Leventhal wrote a latency and throughput DTrace script for illumos, but here's a version modified for FreeBSD.

```
#pragma D option quiet
inline uint32_t BIO_READ = 1;
inline uint32_t BIO_WRITE = 2;
this uint64_t delta;
BEGIN
{
 start = timestamp;
}
io:::start
/ args[0] /
{
 ts[args[0]] = timestamp;
}
io:::done
/args[0] && ts[args[0]]/
{
```

```
 this->delta = (timestamp - ts[args[0]]) / 1000;
 this->name = (args[0]->bio_cmd & (BIO_READ | \
      BIO_WRITE)) == BIO_READ ?
 "read " : "write ";
 @q[this->name] = quantize(this->delta);
 @a[this->name] = avg(this->delta);
 @v[this->name] = stddev(this->delta);
 @i[this->name] = count();
 @b[this->name] = sum(args[0]->bio_bcount);
 ts[args[0]] = 0;
}
END
{
 printa(@q);
 normalize(@i, (timestamp - start) / 1000000000);
 normalize(@b, (timestamp - start) / 1000000000 * 1024);

 printf("%-30s %11s %11s %11s %11s\n", "", \
      "avg latency", "stddev", "iops", "throughput");
 printa("%-30s %@9uus %@9uus %@9u/s %@8uk/s\n", @a, \
      @v, @i, @b);
}
```

Run this script several times while your system experiences normal load to get accurate baselines for latency and throughput.

```
# dtrace -s rw.d -c 'sleep 30'
```

The `sleep(1)` command tells the script how long to spend gathering data. The `rw.d` script watches the throughput and latency for this many seconds, then prints out two graphs of read and write performance. At the end you'll get a report like so:

```
...
      avg latency  stddev  iops  throughput
write      1362us  8378us  68/s     4620k/s
read       6943us  5839us   2/s       46k/s
```

Generally speaking, the goal of performance tuning is to improve the numbers you care about without making the other numbers too large. Play with the maximum number of permitted reads and writes of each type, increasing them by 20–100 percent between runs. Make sure you don't hoist these values high enough that your VDEVs go over the per-VDEV limit—or, alternatively, play with the minimums.

The *stddev* (standard deviation) column is especially noteworthy. You might achieve excellent throughput, but find yourself with wildly varying latency. Is massive throughput okay if some of your reads and writes take five seconds to complete? Only you know.

When adjusting read performance, beware of the ARC. If you keep accessing the same file, the kernel uses the in-memory copy rather than re-reading it from disk. To properly test read performance, you must flush commonly used files from the ARC. Either unmount and remount your read-intensive datasets, or just reboot the machine.

Yes, performance tuning and testing is intrusive. There's a reason why most people don't bother doing it. The good news is, ZFS performs pretty well with the default settings.

I/O Queues

ZFS breaks I/O traffic up into five queues: sync reads, async reads, sync writes, async writes, and scrubs. Each has a pair of related sysctls that control the maximum and minimum outstanding requests of that type that can be active concurrently on each storage provider.

Synchronous reads are when the application is asking for the data right now. The application, and possibly the user, is sitting there waiting for that data before it can continue doing its work. *Synchronous writes*, similarly, request that the data get written immediately. Databases—and other applications that want to be sure that they do not do "the next thing" until this data is safely on the disk—request synchronous writes. In ZFS, synchronous writes are done as quickly as possible. This is where the SLOG comes in, a fast dedicated device that synchronous writes can be stored on temporarily, more quickly than storing them normally.

Asynchronous reads are less important, mostly consisting of ZFS's prefetch feature, loading data from the disk in anticipation of your needing it. The application will be notified when ZFS gets around to reading this data in and making it available, rather than explicitly waiting for it. *Asynchronous writes* work in a similar fashion. The application gives some data to ZFS and says, "write this down at some point." ZFS holds the data for asynchronous writes in memory until the next txg is closing, then flush it to the disk. Grouping these writes together and writing them out en masse improves performance.

The maximums and minimums do not apply simultaneously, however. The maximums apply in one set of conditions, while the minimums apply in different conditions. Some of these values for a type of write are identical—both the maximum and minimum for sync reads are set to *10*, for example. This isn't a conflict, only different settings for a different situation.

Sync reads include data requested by a program. Calling up a file in your text editor is a sync read. Control these with the sysctls vfs.zfs.vdev.sync_read_max_active and vfs.zfs.vdev.sync_read_min_active. Each defaults to 10. The user is most likely to notice latency in sync reads. If a user tries to open a file and it takes five seconds instead of 50ms, the user will say the system is slow.

Prefetch requests are async reads; nobody has yet requested that data, but ZFS guesses that the request will arrive soon. If a program reads the first chunk of a file, ZFS has a pretty good idea that a request for the rest of the file is coming soon. Control the number of outstanding async read requests with the sysctls vfs.zfs.vdev.async_read_max_active and vfs.zfs.vdev.async_read_min_active. These default to a maximum of *3* and a minimum of *1*. The purpose of limiting the number of async operations is to ensure that new sync operations do not end up at the back of the line behind a bunch of less important reads. When the number of outstanding operations on the drive drops below the minimum, ZFS adds more work to the queue, with the most important operations being added to the queue first. The order of operations in the queue does not change.

Sync writes are used where a program uses the fsync(2) system call. These requests go straight to the ZIL, either on the data storage providers or on a separate SLOG. These writes are the most important operation, as the calling application is waiting for the operation to finish before it continues. Tuning this value too low decreases throughput and increases latency. Writes in ZFS are usually batched, so take advantage of the write head being in the correct position to write as much data as possible at once. However, if the number of operations to queue is too high, sync reads must wait for the already queued writes to finish, which can negatively impact system responsiveness. The sysctls vfs.zfs.vdev.sync_write_max_active and vfs.zfs.vdev.sync_write_min_active control how many of these requests may be pending per provider at any time. Both default to *10*.

Async writes are normal traffic that doesn't traverse the ZIL. Async writes sit in a txg, then get committed en masse. The sysctls vfs.zfs.vdev.async_write_max_active and vfs.zfs.vdev.async_write_min_active control how many outstanding async write requests can be simultaneously active on a single storage provider. The default maximum is *10* and the minimum *1*.

Scrub processes have their own queues, controlling how many outstanding I/O requests can be active on a pool simultaneously. The sysctls vfs.zfs.vdev.scrub_max_active, with a default of *2*, and vfs.zfs.vdev.scrub_min_active, with a default of *1*, control this queue. Tuning these knobs adjusts how a scrub impacts system load. A higher queue depth makes the scrub complete sooner, but queues other operations behind the scrub operations.

How ZFS uses these limits depends on the number of outstanding requests permitted.

Per-VDEV Requests

To know how ZFS will schedule activity, you must know how many outstanding requests can go to each of the system's VDEVs. Consider the maximum number of requests of each type per storage provider (usually a disk), as given by the sysctls from the previous section.

sync read maximum: 10
async reads maximum: 3
sync write maximum: 10
async writes maximum: 10
scrub maximum: 2

A disk with the maximum number of simultaneous requests possible would have 35 outstanding requests. A 10-disk VDEV could have 350 simultaneous outstanding requests, where a 29-disk VDEV could have 1015 simultaneous outstanding requests.

Looking at the requests of each type, you'll see that this is a fairly balanced plan. Synchronous and asynchronous writes get their own queues, so your writes won't overload the ZIL. You get as many reads as asynchronous writes. File-level prefetch is turned down so ZFS' guesses on the data your programs will want won't overwhelm traffic programs actively request.

Changing these values adjusts how ZFS can distribute requests. You want your system balanced towards writing data? Increase the maximum number of async writes. You want fast scrubs? Lift the scrub request ceiling.

You cannot increase your hardware speed by cranking these settings, however. The existing limits can more than saturate a 5400 RPM SATA hard drive. High-end storage devices, where you have separate hardware for reading and writing, can probably handle slightly higher values. Even then, you'll hit the maximum capacity fairly soon.

For solid-state storage, like SSDs, where the number of IOPS can be much greater than with spinning disks, performance can be improved by increasing all of these tunables. In order to get the most performance out of your device, you must give it enough work to keep busy, but at the same time, not so much work that it takes too long to get to an important request added to the end of the queue. Use the DTrace scripts provided earlier in this chapter to measure latency under loads and adjust as necessary.

If you have super-duper hardware and raise the limits too high, though, you'll hit the per-VDEV limits, changing everything.

Scheduling Large VDEVs

ZFS has two scheduling systems: one for use when the system permits many outstanding I/O requests, and another for when the system doesn't. How many is many? That depends on your VDEVs and your host.

The sysctl vfs.zfs.vdev.max_active gives a flag level where ZFS changes scheduling algorithms. FreeBSD's default is 1000. For most hosts, in the default configuration, this means that you can have up to 28 disks in a VDEV before switching algorithms. If you alter your I/O queues, you change the math.

Hitting the limit means that ZFS changes how it schedules. Rather than using the maximum values as a ceiling, it permits each disk a number of outstanding requests equal to the minimum values.

sync read minimum: 10
async reads minimum: 3
sync write minimum: 10
async writes minimum: 1
scrub minimum: 1

This means that each disk gets at least 25 outstanding requests. The system can support up to 1000 outstanding requests by default, so any additional requests get assigned in priority order.

If you have more than 40 storage providers in a single VDEV, even the minimums exceed the total permitted on the system. Either change vfs.zfs.vdev.max_active to permit more requests or, preferably, rearrange your VDEVs to contain a sane number of storage providers.

Asynchronous Writes and Transaction Group Sizes

Asynchronous writes work slightly differently. When the system is mostly idle, and doesn't have much to write, the system creates a single asynchronous write request. (Technically, the minimum number is the sysctl vfs.zfs.vdev.async_write_min_active, but there's really no reason to turn this above 1.) Data that's in memory and waiting to be written to disk is called "dirty data." As transaction groups increase in size and frequency, ZFS schedules more and more concurrent writes. When the system hits the maximum number of write requests, as defined by the vfs.zfs.vdev.async_write_max_active sysctl, it starts artificially slowing responses to write requests.

The sysctls vfs.zfs.vdev.async_write_active_min_dirty_percent and vfs.zfs.vdev.async_write_active_max_dirty_percent control how ZFS adds write requests. These are percentages of the allowed dirty data on the system—the maximum size of a txg, or the value of the sysctl vfs.zfs.dirty_data_max. At the minimum percentage and below, the system uses the minimum number of write requests, leaving more bandwidth for reads. At the maximum percentage and above, the system uses the maximum number of write requests to try to keep up with the amount of data that needs to be written. The number of requests scales linearly between them.

By default, the minimum percentage is *30* and the maximum is *60*. The minimum number of async write requests is *1*, and the maximum is *10*. How does this play out?

Assume a host has vfs.zfs.dirty_data_max set to 1 GB, because it makes the math easy. One txg can be only 1 GB in size. If a host has up to 300 MB of data ready to write (30 percent of 1 GB), it uses a single write request. Each 30 MB of dirty data over 300 adds another write request. If the host has 600 MB of data ready to write (60 percent of 1 GB), it queues 10 write requests.

In an ideal world, where the system is cruising along at normal load, the size of a txg should go somewhere between the minimum and maximum size. Our host with vfs.zfs.dirty_data_max should have an amount of dirty data around 450 MB, plus or minus 150.

Maybe your VDEVs can handle more than 10 commands queued to the disk, so you want to increase the vfs.zfs.vdev.async_write_max_active sysctl. Increasing this sysctl beyond what your hardware can handle causes increased latency, so be sure to monitor the effects of any changes under normal load. Changing the maximum number of outstanding write requests impacts how quickly the system creates write requests, but it doesn't affect the percentages.

The percentages given are suitable for most loads, but if your system's latency fluctuates, you might investigate the number of operations and the amount of latency.

```
#pragma D option aggpack
#pragma D option quiet

fbt::vdev_queue_max_async_writes:entry
{
 self->spa = args[0];
}
fbt::vdev_queue_max_async_writes:return
/self->spa && self->spa->spa_name == $$1/
{
 @ = lquantize(args[1], 0, 30, 1);
}

tick-1s
{
 printa(@);
 clear(@);
}

fbt::vdev_queue_max_async_writes:return
/self->spa/
{
 self->spa = 0;
}
```

Run this script with `dtrace`, giving it the name of a pool as an argument.

```
# dtrace -s q.d zroot
```

You'll get bar graphs every second, displaying current latency and the number of operations.

If you have varying latency and number of operations, you might decrease vfs.zfs.vdev.async_write_active_min_dirty_percent so that the system fires up additional write requests more quickly. You could also increase the maximum percentage in vfs.zfs.vdev.async_write_active_min_dirty_percent, or increase the amount of dirty data permitted on the system.

Hardware is all unique. If you dive this far into ZFS tuning, you must twiddle these dials and see what they do on your particular hardware.

Throttling Writes

Programs that ask the kernel to write to disk won't proceed until the kernel acknowledges the write request. There are exceptions—in a multithreaded program, the write request probably blocks only a single thread. Applications that run in multiple simultaneous processes, like Apache, will probably only have a single process block on I/O. Still, in general, every program or some part of the program blocks on I/O until the kernel acknowledges the write request.

In the most common situation, OpenZFS acknowledges receipt of data as soon as the data is in a transaction group ready to write to disk. This works well—until the underlying hardware can't keep up with the write requests. While you can't log every packet on a saturated gigabit line on a SATA-I drive, some people insist on trying.

When the storage providers start lagging behind the write requests, OpenZFS artificially delays acknowledging receipt of data. The requesting program won't continue until the write request is acknowledged. It hangs for a few milliseconds, or longer if needed. Effectively, when a program pushes the kernel too hard, the kernel shoves back.

A one-line DTrace script can identify if your system is delaying writes.

```
# dtrace -n fbt::dsl_pool_need_dirty_delay:return'{ @
[args[1] == 0 ? "no delay" : "delay"] = count(); }'
```

Run this script during a performance issue. Let it gather data for "a while"—anything from several seconds to a couple minutes. Hit CTRL-C to quit. You'll get the number of artificially delayed writes and the number of not-delayed writes. If only a small fraction of your writes are delayed, your performance problems lie elsewhere.

FreeBSD includes sysctls to tweak the delay values, or adjust latency so it's more consistent, but if your hardware is backing up, you're clearly trying to stuff too much data through your storage I/O. Split your writes between more devices, add hardware, or improve your hardware.

Scrub and Resilver Performance

Anyone who has worked in a large enterprise has suffered through maintenance window policies that aren't quite so well suited to modern hardware. Lucas has more than once delayed replacing a failed hot-swappable hard drive during working hours, because the corporate maintenance policy declared that Sunday morning was the only time such maintenance could be performed[23]. If you're stuck with this sort of policy, it's vital that resilvers and scrubs finish quickly so that you can get on with your day.

Scrubs and resilvers have built-in rate limiting so that these operations don't interfere with normal operations. If any other process wants I/O, these maintenance operations are delayed. Accelerating scrubs and resilvers means disabling that rate limiting.

The rate limiting is a sysctl that gives an amount of time to put between each I/O operation for that process. This rate limiting only kicks in while the disk is not idle.

The delay is measured in system ticks. The number of ticks in a second is controlled by the kern.hz sysctl. This defaults to *1000*, although many virtual machines and laptop owners might set this to *100* in the hopes of improving performance.

What exactly does "not idle" mean? The disk must have no activity for a number of ticks equal to the vfs.zfs.scan_idle sysctl.

The sysctl vfs.zfs.resilver_delay controls this artificial lag for resilvers, while vfs.zfs.scrub_delay handles scrubs. By default scrubs

23 Not that Lucas remembers every single minute lost to such daftness. Or keeps a list of people whose policies cost him weekends. Or is waiting for Kneecappers Inc.'s formal response to his Request For Quote.

wait for four ticks between operations, while resilvers lag for two. If ZFS sleeps for four ticks between each I/O, the maximum IOPS generated by a scrub on a non-idle pool would be 250 IOPS (1000 ticks per second divided by four ticks per operation). Other processes get a chance to perform I/O during these pauses. Running those operations further delays the scrub or resilver.

Other OpenZFS consumers, such as illumos, often use 100 ticks per second. FreeBSD thus delays only one-tenth as long as most other operating systems. This was probably an oversight rather than a deliberate design decision.

To eliminate the scrub or resilver delay, set these to *0*, giving your maintenance the same priority as any other process. Remember, these delays only trigger if there is other activity on the pool.

You can control how much data the scrub sends to the I/O scheduler. Increasing the queue depth gives the ZFS I/O scheduler an opportunity to run more effectively. The sysctl vfs.zfs.top_maxinflight controls the scrub I/O queue depth. It defaults to *32*, but some people raise this as high as *2048*. Increasing this too far will exhaust system RAM, so monitor your system closely as you tune scrubs.

Each txg sets a minimum amount of time it spends on resilvering. By default, a txg spends a minimum of 3000 milliseconds on resilvering. The vfs.zfs.resilver_min_time_ms controls how much time the transaction group spends on resilvering I/O. This value is ignored when there's no resilvering going on.

No matter what you do, eventually you'll reach your hardware's limits for your workload. Rearranging bottlenecks is like rearranging deck chairs on a cruise ship. On some ships, you make space for a nice game of shuffleboard. If the ship is the Titanic, though, no amount of shifting resources will keep you afloat.

Chapter 9: Tuning

A sysadmin learning ZFS usually spends time scratching her head over ZFS' space use. Combining pooled storage, datasets, snapshots, and clones, makes ZFS space utilization very complicated, demanding a whole chapter in *FreeBSD Mastery: ZFS*. When you start mucking with the **recordsize** and **volblocksize** properties for databases and zvols, space utilization can swerve straight into the Twilight Zone.

The **volblocksize** property gives the size of a storage block on a zvol. The block size should represent the block size of the filesystem used on the zvol. The default **volblocksize** is 8 KB, which would hold two 4 KB or 16 512-byte filesystem sectors.

The **recordsize** property gives the maximum size of a logical block in a ZFS filesystem dataset. The default **recordsize** is 128 KB, which comes to 32 sectors on a disk with 4 KB sectors, or 256 sectors on a disk with 512 byte sectors. The maximum record size was increased to 1 MB with the introduction of the `large_blocks` feature flag in 2015. Many database engines prefer smaller blocks, such as 4 KB or 8 KB. It makes sense to change the **recordsize** on datasets dedicated to such files. Even if you don't change the **recordsize**, ZFS automatically sizes records as needed. Writing a 16 KB file should take up only 16 KB of space (plus metadata and redundancy space), not waste an entire 128 KB record.

Interactions between block size and RAID-Z mean that the server's disks can suddenly fill up, even though they have only 25 percent of the data you'd expect them to hold.

Understanding why requires diving deeper into how ZFS allocates blocks.

ZFS Stripe Allocation

Stripes are made up of sectors on the physical disk (or other provider, such as a GELI). If your disk has 4 KB sectors, allocating 128 KB requires 32 physical sectors.

Zpools store all parity information in disk sectors, or blocks. Each level of parity requires a block for each stripe. A RAID-Z3 pool needs three blocks for parity information for each chunk of disk allocated.

RAID-Z pools always allocate blocks in multiples of the parity level plus one. That is, RAID-Z1 allocates two blocks at a time, RAID-Z2 three blocks at a time, and RAID-Z3 four blocks at a time. This helps ZFS prevent fragmentation and reduces the risk of wasting more space. If a stripe doesn't need that much space, ZFS pads it out to fill the entire allocation. For usual stripe sizes, an extra sector or two per file doesn't matter. RAID-Z allocates in consistent-sized blocks so that when a block is freed, it can be easily reused.

Consider allocating 8 KB of space on a RAID-Z2. While 8 KB requires only four sectors, RAID-Z2 allocates only in multiples of three, so it gets six blocks. You erase that file, and allocate for a 4 KB file in the same sectors. This 4 KB file needs only three blocks. If RAID-Z didn't pad to multiples of N+1, you'd get a single unused disk block between the 4 KB file and the next file. This lone block, an orphaned sector, could never be used.

Write and delete and write a bunch of files of different sizes, and pretty soon your disk has a whole bunch of free space—but it's all in unusable one-block chunks. Your disk would be paralyzed.

Each file also needs other metadata to attach it to the ZFS tree, giving the blocks containing the file, their hashes, and such. Each such metadata block contains the information on many files, and can be ignored for this discussion.

This all seems straightforward and unworrisome, but let's see how these facts interact with filesystems using 4 KB and 512-byte sectors. In all of these examples, we're writing a single 8 KB block, either for a zvol or a database.

Mirrors and Stripes

Mirrors and stripes need blocks of metadata to attach them to the ZFS tree, but they don't require any additional redundancy blocks. Our 8 KB file uses two 4 KB or 16 512-byte disk sectors.

RAID-Z1

On a RAID-Z1 pool with 4 KB blocks, our 8 KB of data takes two blocks. We also need a block for parity data, for a total of three blocks. A RAID-Z1 pool allocates blocks in multiples of two (the parity level plus one), so this gets rounded up to four. Assume you have a three-drive RAID-Z1. If the disks have 4 KB blocks, this means you can only fill the physical disks half full of data, rather than the two-thirds full you'd expect from a three-disk RAID-Z1. Padding eats the rest of that space.

If this same three-drive RAID-Z1 pool uses disks with 512 byte blocks, that same 8 KB takes 16 blocks. We need one parity block, for a total of 17 blocks. The allocation must be divisible by two, so the pool allocates one block for padding, bringing the total up to 18 blocks. You can fill this pool up to 88 percent full of 8 KB blocks.

RAID-Z2

Our 8 KB of data again takes two blocks on a RAID-Z2 pool with 4 KB blocks. We'll need two blocks for parity data, for a total of four blocks. A RAID-Z2 pool allocates blocks in multiples of three (the parity level plus one), so this gets rounded up to six blocks. On a four-drive RAID-Z2, you'd expect to be able to fill your disks half full of real data.

If you fill the pool with 8 KB files, though, you get only about 33 percent full before padding eats up your space.

On a pool with 512 byte blocks, 8 KB of data gets 16 blocks. Two blocks of parity data brings us to 18 blocks. ZFS reserves three blocks at a time, so we don't need any padding at all. You can completely fill this pool with 8 KB blocks.

RAID-Z3

On a ZFS with 4 KB filesystem sectors, the data itself requires two sectors. This pool uses triple parity, so you'll need three disk sectors for parity data. This is a total of five sectors. ZFS allocates sectors only in chunks of parity level plus one. RAID-Z3 lets you allocate sectors in multiples of four, so ZFS allocates eight sectors for this 8 KB of data. Eight sectors is 32 KB. You cannot fill this zvol more than 25 percent full. You could completely fill a 200 GB zvol, so long as the pool has 800 GB of physical space for it.

On a ZFS with 512 byte filesystem sectors, the data itself requires 16 sectors. It needs another three sectors for parity data, for a total of 19 sectors. As allocations must be in multiples of four, this write gets allocated 20 filesystem sectors. Twenty sectors is 10 KB, giving you 80 percent efficiency.

Striped Mirrors

Striped mirrors do not need any parity data. ZFS copies the data wholesale to multiple storage providers. Striped mirrors don't pad data to fit allocation sizes. A striped mirror is the most efficient place to store data, but it has a different data protection model than RAID-Z.

Three-way mirrors give similar data protection to RAID-Z2—you can lose two drives from each VDEV without losing any data—but you get only 33 percent of the total space.

Changing the allocation size

Change `recordsize` or `volblocksize` to 4 KB changes the calculations. A smaller stripe size means more parity, which possibly means more empty padding.

Look at our sample 8 KB write on RAID-Z3. It gets broken up into two stripes. On a zvol with 4 KB blocks, each stripe needs four sectors, again giving you 25 percent space efficiency. With 512-byte blocks, each stripe needs 11 blocks, which gets rounded up to 12. You'll get about 66 percent space efficiency.

The interaction among the stripe size (`volblocksize`), parity, and padding is why you don't have to perform these calculations with filesystem datasets. A stripe size of 128 KB reduces allocation padding to mere noise.

Recommendations

Before setting up a system for databases or zvols, carefully consider the storage beneath the data storage pool. With the common `recordsize` setting of 8 KB we strongly recommend, in order: a mirrored stripe pool, a four-drive RAID-Z2 pool, or a three-drive RAID-Z pool.

If you're using zvols with a `volblocksize` of 4 KB to support virtual machines, your choices are more limited. Mirrored stripe pools allow you maximum space efficiency, while all other sizes cause at least some space loss due to padding. Mirrors also have a great IOPS advantage over RAID-Z.

Databases and ZFS

Many ZFS features are highly advantageous for databases. Every DBA wants fast, easy, and efficient replication, snapshots, clones, tunable caches, and pooled storage. While ZFS is designed as a general-purpose filesystem, you can tune it to make your databases fly.

Databases usually consist of more than one type of file, and since each has different characteristics and usage patterns, each requires different tuning. We'll discuss MySQL and PostgreSQL in particular, but the principles apply to any database software.

The most important tuning you can perform for a database is the dataset block size, through the `recordsize` property. The ZFS `recordsize` for any file that might be overwritten needs to match the block size used by the application.

Tuning the block size also avoids write amplification. Write amplification happens when changing a small amount of data requires writing a large amount of data. Suppose you must change 8 KB in the middle of a 128 KB block. ZFS must read the 128 KB, modify 8 KB somewhere in it, calculate a new checksum, and write the new 128 KB block. ZFS is a copy-on-write filesystem, so it would wind up writing a whole new 128 KB block just to change that 8 KB. You don't want that. Now multiply this by the number of writes your database makes. Write amplification eviscerates performance.

While this sort of optimization isn't necessary for many of us, for a high-performance system it might be invaluable. It can also affect the life of SSDs and other flash-based storage that can handle a limited volume of writes over their lifetime. Of course the different database engines don't make this easy, and each has different needs. Journals, binary replication logs, error and query logs, and other miscellaneous files also require different tuning.

Before creating a dataset with a small `recordsize`, be sure you understand the interaction between VDEV type and space utilization. In some situations, disks with the smaller 512-byte sector size can provide better storage efficiency. It is entirely possible you may be better off with a separate pool specifically for your database, with the main pool for your other files.

For high-performance systems, use mirrors rather than any type of RAID-Z. Yes, for resiliency you probably want RAID-Z. Choose your pain.[24]

All Databases

Enabling lz4 compression on a database can, unintuitively, actually decrease latency. Compressed data can be read more quickly from the physical media, as there is less to read, which can result in shorter transfer times. With lz4's early abort feature, the worst case is only a few milliseconds slower than opting out of compression, but the benefits are usually quite significant. This is why ZFS uses lz4 compression for all of its own metadata and for the L2ARC. In the near future when the Compressed ARC feature lands in OpenZFS, enabling compression on the dataset will also allow more data to be kept in the ARC, the fastest cache in ZFS.

In a production case study done by Delphix, a database server with 768 GB of RAM went from using more than 90 percent of its memory to cache a database to using only 446 GB to cache 1.2 TB of compressed data. Compressing the in-memory cache resulted in a significant performance improvement. As the machine could not support any more RAM, compression was the only way to improve.

ZFS metadata can also affect databases. When a database is rapidly changing, writing out two or three copies of the metadata for each change can take up a significant number of the available IOPS of the backing storage. Normally, the quantity of metadata is relatively small compared to the default 128 KB record size. Databases work better with small record sizes, though. Keeping three copies of the metadata can cause as much disk activity, or more, than writing actual data to the pool.

---

24 Sysadmins don't get to choose between the Lady and the Tiger. We get to choose between Angry Tiger and Hungry Tiger.

Newer versions of OpenZFS also contain a `redundant_metadata` property, which defaults to *all*. This is the original behavior from previous versions of ZFS. However, this property can also be set to *most*, which causes ZFS to reduce the number of copies of some types of metadata that it keeps.

Depending on your needs and workload, allowing the database engine to manage caching might be better. ZFS defaults to caching much or all of the data from your database in the ARC, while the database engine keeps its own cache, resulting in wasteful double caching. Setting the `primarycache` property to *metadata* rather than the default *all* tells ZFS to avoid caching actual data in the ARC. The `secondarycache` property similarly controls the L2ARC.

Depending on the access pattern and the database engine, ZFS may already be more efficient. Use a tool like `zfsmon` from the zfs-tools package to monitor the ARC cache hit ratio, and compare it to that of the database's internal cache.

Once the Compressed ARC feature is available, it might be wise to consider reducing the size of the database's internal cache, and instead letting ZFS handle the caching. The ARC might be able to fit significantly more data in the same amount of RAM than your database can.

MySQL – InnoDB/XtraDB

InnoDB became the default storage engine in MySQL 5.5 and has significantly different characteristics than the previously used MyISAM engine. Percona's XtraDB, also used by MariaDB, is similar to InnoDB. Both InnoDB and XtraDB use a 16 KB block size, so the ZFS dataset that contains the actual data files should have its `recordsize` property set to match. We also recommend using MySQL's `innodb_one_file_per_table` setting to keep the InnoDB data for each table in a separate file, rather than grouping it all into a single ibdata file. This makes snapshots more useful and allows more selective restoration or rollback.

Store different types of files on different datasets. The data files need 16 KB block size, lz4 compression and reduced metadata. You might see performance gains from caching only metadata, but this also disables prefetch. Experiment and see how your environment behaves.

```
# zfs create -o recordsize=16k -o compress=lz4 \
     -o redundant_metadata=most \
     -o primarycache=metadata mypool/var/db/mysql
```

The primary MySQL logs compress best with `gzip`, and don't need caching in memory.

```
# zfs create -o compress=gzip1 -o primarycache=none \
     mysql/var/log/mysql
```

The replication log works best with lz4 compression.

```
# zfs create -o compress=lz4 \
     mypool/var/log/mysql/replication
```

Tell MySQL to use these datasets with these *`/usr/local/etc/my.cnf`* settings.

```
data_path=/var/db/mysql
log_path=/var/log/mysql
binlog_path=/var/log/mysql/replication
```

You can now initialize your database and start loading data.

MySQL – MyISAM

Many MySQL applications still use the older MyISAM storage engine, either because of its simplicity or just because they have not been converted to using InnoDB.

MyISAM uses an 8 KB block size. The dataset record size should be set to match. The dataset layout should otherwise be the same as for InnoDB.

PostgreSQL

ZFS can support very large and fast PostgreSQL systems, if tuned properly. Don't initialize your database until you've created the needed datasets

PostgreSQL defaults to using 8 KB storage blocks for everything. If you change PostgreSQL's block size, you must change the dataset size to match.

On a default FreeBSD install, PostgreSQL goes in */usr/local/pgsql/data*. For a big install, you probably have a separate pool for that data. Here I'm using the pool *pgsql* for PostgreSQL.

```
# zfs set mountpoint=/usr/local/pgsql pgsql
# zfs create pgsql/data
```

Now we have a chicken-and-egg problem. PostgreSQL's database initialization routine expects to create its own directory tree, but we want particular subdirectories to have their own datasets. The easiest way to do this is to let PostgreSQL initialize, and then create datasets and move the files.

```
# /usr/local/etc/rc.d/postgresql oneinitdb
```

The initialization routine creates databases, views, schemas, configuration files, and all the other components of a high-end database. Now you can create datasets for the special parts.

PostgreSQL stores databases in */usr/local/pgsql/data/base*. The Write Ahead Log, or *WAL*, lives in */usr/local/pgsql/data/pg_xlog*. Move both of these out of the way.

```
# cd /usr/local/pgsql/data
# mv base base-old
# mv pg_xlog pg_xlog-old
```

Both of these use an 8 KB block size, and you would want to snapshot them separately, so create a dataset for each. As with MySQL, tell the ARC to cache only the metadata. Also tell these datasets to bias throughput over latency with the `logbias` property.

```
# zfs create -o recordsize=8k \
      -o redundant_metadata=most \
      -o primarycache=metadata logbias=throughput \
      pgsql/data/pg_xlog
# zfs create -o recordsize=8k \
      -o redundant_metadata=most \
      -o primarycache=metadata logbias=throughput \
      pgsql/data/base
```

Copy the contents of the original directories into the new datasets.

```
# cp -Rp base-old/* base
# cp -Rp pg_xlog-old/* pg_xlog
```

You can now start PostgreSQL.

Tuning for File Size

ZFS is designed to be a good general-purpose filesystem. If you have a ZFS system serving as file server for a typical office, you don't really have to tune for file size. If you know what size of files you're going to have, though, you can make changes to improve performance.

Small Files

When creating many small files at high speed in a system without a SLOG, ZFS spends a significant amount of time waiting for the files and metadata to finish flushing to stable storage.

If you are willing to risk the loss of any new files created in the last five seconds (or more if your vfs.zfs.txg.timeout is higher), setting the `sync` property to *disabled* tells ZFS to treat all writes as asynchronous. Even if an application asks that it not be told that the write is complete until the file is safe, ZFS returns immediately and writes the file along with the next regularly scheduled txg.

A high-speed SLOG lets you store those tiny files both synchronously and quickly.

Big Files

ZFS recently added support for blocks larger than 128 KB via the `large_block` feature. If you're storing many large files, certainly consider this. The default maximum block size is 1 MB.

Theoretically, you can use block sizes larger than 1 MB. Very few systems have extensively tested this, however, and the interaction with the kernel memory allocation subsystem has not been tested under prolonged use. You can try really large record sizes, but be sure to file a bug report when everything goes sideways. The sysctl vfs.zfs.max_recordsize controls the maximum block size.

Once you activate `large_blocks` (or any other feature), the pool can no longer be used by hosts that do not support the feature. Deactivate the feature by destroying any datasets that have ever had their **`recordsize`** set to larger than 128 KB.

Storage systems struggle to balance latency and throughput. ZFS uses the **`logbias`** property to decide which way it should lean. ZFS uses a **`logbias`** of *latency* by default, so that data is quickly synched to disk, allowing databases and other applications to continue working. When dealing with large files, changing the **`logbias`** property to *throughput* might result in better performance. You must do your own testing and decide which setting is right for your workload.

The Worst of Both Worlds: Bittorrent

Bittorrent combines the worst parts of large files and the worst parts of small files all in one convenient package. Bittorrent's out-of-order write pattern can cause a great deal of dataset fragmentation. Plus, Bittorrent's 16 KB block size can lead to write amplification if the **`recordsize`** of the dataset isn't also 16 KB.

The best solution to both of these issues is to actually have two datasets. The dataset where the files are stored during downloading uses the smaller record size.

```
# zfs create -o recordsize=16k \
      -o redundant_metadata=most -o compress=off \
      mypool/torrents/in-progress
```

The dataset where you store completed torrents should have a larger block size. Moving files from one to the other defragments the files, resulting in improved read performance and avoiding pool fragmentation. Most torrent clients support using a separate directory for in-progress downloads, so this should not even require any action on your part aside from creating the two datasets.

If you download large files, like operating system ISOs, you might also consider using a `recordsize` of 1 MB to further increase performance and amortize metadata and redundancy.

```
# zfs create -o recordsize=1m mypool/torrents
```

Tell your torrent client about these directories and you'll be ready to go.

Short Stroking

Regular spinning disks have specific characteristics that can cause uneven performance. Reads and writes to the beginning of the disk can be significantly faster (higher throughput) than writes later on the disk. The slowest aspect of a regular spinning disk is *seek time*, the time it takes for the drive to physically reposition the read/write head over the sector you want to read or write. When data is scattered all over the disk, this can significantly decrease performance.

Short Stroking is the process of using only a small subset of a disk's capacity, usually a partition of only the fastest 10–30% of a disk. Now that the head only ever has to travel over a small portion of the disk's surface, the average seek time will be significantly less. In the future, if more storage space is required, the partition can simply be resized and ZFS will grow the pool. Remember that running ZFS low on disk space increases fragmentation, which can be much worse for performance than a higher average seek time.

You now have the tools to configure your datasets, pools, and hardware in the best possible manner. Now let's poke at some more obscure corners of ZFS.

Chapter 10: ZFS Potpourri

This chapter covers small topics that didn't quite fit anywhere else.

Splitting Mirrors

Combining storage into pools is one of ZFS' core features. But ZFS lets you perform the same action in reverse—splitting mirrored pools into multiple identical pools. If you want to more literally clone a machine, or pull off a copy of a mirror to run a backup, or perform some other sort of mad computer science, `zpool split` is your friend.

We'll demonstrate adding disks to a mirrored pool, then split the pool into duplicates. You could perform the same task in reverse: pool the disks off a mirror, then add them back when you're done with the duplicate. We recommend maintaining at least two providers in each mirror VDEV at all times, however.

Make Mirrors Deeper

A mirror's depth describes how many copies of data the mirror includes. This pool, a typical striped mirror, contains two mirrors of two disks each.

```
# zpool status db
...
NAME          STATE    READ WRITE CKSUM
 db           ONLINE      0     0     0
  mirror-0    ONLINE      0     0     0
   gpt/zfs0   ONLINE      0     0     0
   gpt/zfs1   ONLINE      0     0     0
  mirror-1    ONLINE      0     0     0
   gpt/zfs2   ONLINE      0     0     0
   gpt/zfs3   ONLINE      0     0     0
```

I want to make this pool deeper, adding an additional disk to each VDEV. Use the `zpool attach` command with the pool name, a device already in the target VDEV, and the new device.

```
# zpool attach db gpt/zfs1 gpt/zfs4
# zpool attach db gpt/zfs3 gpt/zfs5
```

In between running these two commands, the pool has one mirror of three devices and one mirror of two devices. At the end, the mirror looks like this.

```
NAME            STATE     READ WRITE CKSUM
 db             ONLINE       0     0     0
  mirror-0      ONLINE       0     0     0
   gpt/zfs0     ONLINE       0     0     0
   gpt/zfs1     ONLINE       0     0     0
   gpt/zfs4     ONLINE       0     0     0
  mirror-1      ONLINE       0     0     0
   gpt/zfs2     ONLINE       0     0     0
   gpt/zfs3     ONLINE       0     0     0
   gpt/zfs5     ONLINE       0     0     0
```

Once the pool finishes resilvering the drives, you can split the pool.

Splitting the Pool

Use the `zpool split` command to pull a device from each VDEV to create the new pool. The command has two mandatory arguments: the name of the pool you want to split and a name for the newly created pool. Here we split the pool *db*, creating an identical copy in the pool *db2*.

```
# zpool split db db2
```

ZFS removes the device most recently added to each mirror to create a new pool. Splitting a pool does not automatically import the new pool. Once you import it, the split pool looks like this.

```
# zpool status db2
...
NAME          STATE    READ WRITE CKSUM
db2           ONLINE      0     0     0
  gpt/zfs4    ONLINE      0     0     0
  gpt/zfs5    ONLINE      0     0     0
```

This pool contains two striped disks.

In the original pool, the striped pair of three-way mirrors has become a striped pair of two-disk mirrors.

If you're keeping this split-off pool around for any length of time, you should add more disks to create proper mirrors. You might not add another set of disks if you're pulling backups off of these drives, though.

SnapSpec

Snapshots are great—but they breed like tribbles™. Once you're accustomed to using snapshots to deal with system administration issues, you'll find yourself dealing with disk space shortages because of all the snapshots you have. Removing a single snapshot is easy.

```
# zfs destroy mypool/dataset@snapshotname
```

But what if you want to destroy 10 snapshots at once? Identifying each snapshot and specifying each on the command line is incredibly tedious.

ZFS lets you identify multiple neighboring snapshots with a *snapspec*. You can't use a snapspec to specify multiple disparate snapshots, but if you want to blow away daily snapshots @monday through @saturday, a snapspec is your friend.

Any time you use a snapspec, we recommend first running your command with `-n` and `-v`. The `-v` flag tells zfs(1) to print what the command does in more detail. The `-n` tells it to not to actually do anything. Combined, they say "give me more detail on exactly what this command will do." As you can assign arbitrary snapshot names, it's best to verify that a needed but forgotten snapshot won't be caught up in a snapshot massacre. Once you know exactly which snapshots the command will destroy, rerun the command without the `-n`.

Snapshot Range

The most basic snapspec is *fromsnap%tosnap*. It destroys every snapshot between the two indicated, including themselves:

```
# zfs destroy -vn mypool/dataset@one%three
would destroy mypool/dataset@one
would destroy mypool/dataset@two
would destroy mypool/dataset@three
```

Did you slip a @beforeUpgrade snapshot in between the numbered snaps? This is why you use `-n` first.

Specify by Age

You can use *@%foo* to destroy snapshot @foo and anything older than it.

```
# zfs destroy -vn mypool/dataset@%four
would destroy mypool/dataset@one
would destroy mypool/dataset@two
would destroy mypool/dataset@three
would destroy mypool/dataset@four
```

Similarly, use *@foo%* to destroy @foo and anything newer than itself:

```
# zfs destroy -vn mypool/dataset@six%
would destroy mypool/dataset@six
would destroy mypool/dataset@seven
would destroy mypool/dataset@eight
would destroy mypool/dataset@nine
would destroy mypool/dataset@ten
```

That's much easier than re-entering each snapshot name.

Snapshot Slaughter

Sometimes, you want to destroy all the snapshots. Use @% to burn it all down.

```
# zfs destroy -vn mypool/dataset@%
would destroy mypool/dataset@one
would destroy mypool/dataset@two
...
would destroy mypool/dataset@ten
```

Now you can start accumulating snapshots all over again.

If you've taken recursive snapshots, you probably want to burn the whole tree down. Add `-R` to eradicate snapshots from a dataset and all its children. Here, we've finished the upgrade and think we're happy with the results.

```
# zfs destroy -nvR pgsql/data@%
would destroy pgsql/data@beforeupgrade
would destroy pgsql/data/base@beforeupgrade
would destroy pgsql/data/pg_xlog@beforeupgrade
```

But, you know ... we think we'll hold on to those backups just a *little* longer.

Recovering Destroyed Pools

There's nothing quite like the moment when you realize, "Wait, that command is a horrible mistake" and you try to stop, but you know that the nerve impulses don't have time to race down from your brain to your hand before your accursed pinky finishes pressing the `ENTER` key.

One place that can happen is when you destroy a ZFS pool. And the ZFS designers were very aware of exactly this syndrome.

The `zpool destroy` command doesn't actually damage any data on the underlying disks. Instead, it marks the pool as destroyed. A `zpool list` skips pools marked as destroyed. If you haven't written to or physically removed the disks underlying the destroyed pool, you can recover the pool. Use the `-D` flag to `zpool import` to view destroyed pools.

```
# zpool import -D
```

You'll get two kinds of responses, for recoverable and non-recoverable pools.

Recoverable Pools

Here's a pool that you can easily recover.

```
# zpool import -D
   pool: db2
   id: 5552158746006792385
  state: ONLINE (DESTROYED)
 action: The pool can be imported using its name or
         numeric identifier.
 config:
      db2         ONLINE
        gpt/zfs4  ONLINE
        gpt/zfs5  ONLINE
```

This destroyed pool, *db2*, looks like a normal, healthy pool. The state says it's DESTROYED, but the output shows the two providers in the pool's single VDEV, and they're both online.

To import a destroyed pool, run `zpool import -D` and give the pool name. Let's reactivate pool *db2*.

```
# zpool import -D db2
```

Other pools are not so easy.

Non-Recoverable Pools

Other destroyed pools look more like this.

```
# zpool import -D
   pool: db
   id: 13121127349626326109
  state: UNAVAIL (DESTROYED)
 status: One or more devices are missing from the
         system.
 action: The pool cannot be imported. Attach the missing
         devices and try again.
   see: http://illumos.org/msg/ZFS-8000-6X
 config:
      db                        UNAVAIL  missing device
        mirror-1                DEGRADED
          6883971156539624736  UNAVAIL  cannot open
          gpt/zfs3              ONLINE
      Additional devices are known to be part of this
      pool, though their exact configuration cannot be
      determined.
```

The pool state here is `UNAVAIL`, meaning you can't import it. The configuration shows that one of the providers is also `UNAVAIL`. ZFS cannot find a storage provider with the ZFS-specific GUID for this pool. Perhaps you've reused that disk, or unplugged it from the chassis.

What's most vexing in this example? This pool is a two-provider mirror. You have a perfectly good copy of the data on the surviving provider. But the pool is incomplete, so no, you can't import it. Go looking for that disk you pulled out.

Another common case is when a pool no longer has a SLOG device. SLOG-suitable hardware normally gets put straight back into use on another pool or discarded. To tell zpool(8) to disregard the missing SLOG and import the pool anyway, use `zpool -m`.

Rename Pool at Recovery

Sometimes you want to rename a pool when you un-destroy it. Perhaps it has the same name as a live pool, or the function of the pool has changed. To rename a pool when you import it, add the new name after the pool's old name. Here we import the destroyed pool *db2*, and rename it *olddb2*.

```
# zpool import -D db2 olddb2
```

It's otherwise the same as renaming an imported pool.

Cloning Machines

ZFS is a perfectly sensible choice for virtual machines. While losing direct access to the disks means that ZFS can't handle error detection for you, features such as snapshots and replication make ZFS worthwhile.

Most virtualization systems offer to clone systems for you, sometimes disguised as a standard template you can deploy. If you copy a disk image containing a ZFS pool to a new virtual machine, though, your virtual machine is a copy of the original. This means that some items that should be globally unique, no longer are. Will this cause problems? Not on a stand-alone virtual machine. If you're going to move disk images between virtual machines, though, you'll want to change the GUID of each VM's pools.

The `guid` property contains a pool's GUID. Here we get the GUID of the pool *db2*.

```
# zpool get guid db2
NAME  PROPERTY  VALUE   SOURCE
db2   guid     5552158746006792385  default
```

To generate a new pool GUID, use `zpool reguid`. Give the pool name as an argument.

```
# zpool reguid db2
# zpool get guid db2
NAME   PROPERTY   VALUE   SOURCE
db2    guid       7662460469377566669   default
```

You can now attach the disk image from one virtual machine to another without making ZFS have a hissy fit.

Giving a pool a new GUID can also help if for some reason zdb(8) cannot find your pool.[25] [26] [27] [28]

Case-Insensitive Filesystem

Some clients (OS X in particular) expect filesystems to be case-insensitive. You can tell a ZFS dataset to be case-insensitive with the `casesensitivity` property.

The `casesensitivity` property defaults to *sensitive*, which is traditional Unix-style case sensitive. If you set it to *mixed*, ZFS can support both case-sensitive and case-insensitive requests. Setting `casesensitivity` to *insensitive* means that ZFS will be completely case-insensitive.

You can set this property only at dataset creation time.

```
# zfs create -o casesensitivity=mixed samba/share
```

To change `casesensitivity` on an existing dataset, create a new dataset with the property set correctly, and then copy the files over.

---

25 This once happened to Jude, but Lucas is certain that it was actually operator error.

26 Actually, Jude thinks it might be related to upgrading a pool from an older version, as it happened recently on two more machines he was running zdb on for writing this chapter of the book

27 Just because you make the same mistake multiple times, Jude, doesn't mean it's not an error.

28 At least Jude provided the solution, so when Lucas inevitably runs into this problem he'll know what to do: curse Jude. For the record, the only mistake Jude made was writing this book with such a... swell guy.

ZFS Deep Dive: zdb(8)

To better understand what's happening inside ZFS, it helps to be able to peek behind the curtain. Examining the internal state of ZFS can help you understand why the system is performing or behaving the way it is. Even if you're not terribly interested in how the sausage is made, this section might contain some points of interest.

Many people read the ZFS chapter of *The Design and Implementation of the FreeBSD Operating System, 2nd Edition* (Addison-Wesley Professional, 2014), to learn about ZFS's internal data structures. While the *D&I* book provides a great deal of information, the ability to study those data structures for actual files on your system can help everything make sense.

The suite of ZFS tools available in FreeBSD includes zdb(8), the ZFS debugger. The zdb(8) man page clearly states that "The output of this command in general reflects the on-disk structure of a ZFS pool, and is inherently unstable. The precise output of most invocations is not documented, a knowledge of ZFS internals is assumed." The output is based on what is on the disk and zdb(8)'s simulation of what's in memory at any given instant. The interpretation is largely left up to the operator. If you really dig into zdb(8), you probably need a copy of *D&I* handy for reference.[29]

The zdb(8) command has a large number of flags. Most all of these can be specified multiple times, each increasing the verbosity of the information.

Block Statistics

The zdb(8) utility can examine the breakdown of how blocks are allocated in the pool. We'll start by examining a very small pool from

29 Hey, we recommend their book, they recommend ours. Or at least buy a round. It works out.

a virtual machine, and then increasingly larger pools. Use the `-b` flag and the pool name to get block statistics for that pool.

Analyzing block statistics takes a lot of memory, as zdb(8) must track every block as it calculates the various statistics. A very large pool might require more memory than the host has, and eventually the kernel's out-of-memory killer will terminate `zdb` in self-defense. Be careful running this on a production system, as zdb(8) can grind the system to a halt.

Let's start with a small one-disk pool from a virtual machine.

```
# zdb -b mypool
Traversing all blocks to verify nothing leaked ...
 925M completed ( 473MB/s) estimated time remaining: 0hr 00min 00sec
  No leaks (block sum matches space maps exactly)
  bp count:            85010
  ganged count:            0
  bp logical:     2159973376    avg:  25408
  bp physical:     897291776    avg:  10555   compression:    2.41
  bp allocated:   1159446528    avg:  13638   compression:    1.86
  bp deduped:              0  ref>1:      0   deduplication:  1.00
  SPA allocated: 1159446528   used:  5.72%

  additional, non-pointer bps of type 0:  5873
  Dittoed blocks on same vdev: 9645
```

The first part of the statistics covers block pointers, the blocks that contain metadata and indexing details for data blocks. The *bp count* field shows how many block pointers the pool has—here, 85,010.

The *bp logical* field shows the total amount of logical space, or the actual file sizes, of those blocks. These block pointers point to 2,159,973,376 bytes, or about 2 GB. The average block pointer handles about 25,408 bytes.

The *bp physical* amount shows how much space these blocks consume on the disk. This is where the advantages of compression show up. While we have about 2 GB of files, this shows we're using about 800 MB of disk space for files. But that's not quite the whole story.

The *bp allocated* number gives the actual real-world disk space consumption. Sector size, padding, and parity mean that we don't actually get all of the savings that compression provided. This server gets a real-world compression factor of 1.86, fitting that 2 GB in roughly 1.1 GB—still significant.

Here's a slightly larger pool from an active server with only a single disk VDEV:

```
bp count:            1877355
bp logical:      40057641984    avg:  21337
bp physical:     36864202240    avg:  19636    compression:   1.09
bp allocated:    40843472896    avg:  21755    compression:   0.98
bp deduped:                0  ref>1:      0  deduplication:   1.00
SPA allocated: 40843472896    used:  8.34%
```

This pool contains a lot of non-compressible data. The *bp physical* entry says that we eke out a compression factor of 1.09. Look further down at the allocated space, though. Once you add in metadata and padding overhead, we actually get 0.98 compression. The compression *almost* compensates for space lost due to metadata.

Let's examine a bigger pool, a four-disk RAID-Z1.

```
bp count:             243197
ganged count:              0
bp logical:      15037198336    avg:  61831
bp physical:     10384008704    avg:  42697    compression:   1.45
bp allocated:    15081398272    avg:  62013    compression:   1.00
bp deduped:                0  ref>1:      0  deduplication:   1.00
SPA allocated: 15081398272    used:  0.19%
```

With a four-disk RAID-Z1, you'd expect to lose 25 percent of your physical space to parity. It has about 15 GB of data, but compression squeezes that down to about 10 GB. Once you look at the allocated space, though, compression and RAID-Z metadata even each other out.

Here's another four-disk RAID-Z1, but with more data:

```
bp count:             8782753
bp logical:      845698973696    avg:  96290
bp physical:     838824515072    avg:  95508    compression:   1.01
bp allocated:   1173701099520    avg: 133637    compression:   0.72
bp deduped:                 0  ref>1:      0  deduplication:   1.00
SPA allocated: 1173701099520   used: 29.70%
```

This stores about 845 GB of data. Once you add in the RAID-Z1 metadata, though, it allocates more than a terabyte.

Detailed Block Statistics

If those numbers didn't make your brain climb out of your ear canal and fling itself to its death, add a second `-b` to get detailed block statistics.

```
# zdb -bb mypool
```

You'll get columns for the number of blocks (BLOCKS), the logical size (LSIZE), physical size (PSIZE), allocated size (ASIZE), average (avg), compression (comp), and percentage of total (%Total), for each different type of block pointer. And there are dozens of different types of block pointer. The output below presents only a few.

```
Blocks  LSIZE  PSIZE  ASIZE    avg  comp  %Total  Type
     9  68.0K  68.0K  68.0K  7.55K  1.00    0.01  ZIL intent log
 70.3K  1.87G   844M  1.01G  14.7K  2.26   93.43  ZFS plain file
 7.12K   9.6M  2.53M  24.7M  3.47K  3.78    2.23  ZFS directory
   272   174K  38.0K   608K  2.23K  4.58    0.05  ZFS user/group used
   244   315K  59.0K  1.38M  5.80K  5.34    0.13  DSL deadlist map
     6  60.0K  11.0K  72.0K  12.0K  5.45    0.01  deferred free
     8  66.0K  10.0K  84.0K  10.5K  6.60    0.01  other
...
 83.0K  2.01G  856M   1.08G  13.3K  2.41  100.00  Total
```

What do each of these block pointer types mean? That's where we point you to *D&I*. Here are a few that might interest you, though.

The last line gives the totals. This pool has about 83,000 blocks for pointers, representing 2.01 GB of data. This data uses 856 MB of logical space, but needs 1.08 GB once ZFS adds in the padding and metadata.

The ZIL gives information about the ZFS intent log's space usage. Remember, even if you don't have a separate ZIL, each pool dedicates space for the ZIL. Our ZIL is using nine blocks, representing 68 KB of data. This information can help you size a separate ZIL, or determine if one is needed.

The *ZFS plain file* and *ZFS directory* lines show the amount of disk space used on files and directory entries. Of the 2.01 GB stored on this pool, files use 70,300 block pointers for 1.87 GB, and 7,120 block pointers for 9.6 MB of directory entries.

This pool uses 272 blocks, or 174 KB, just to keep track of user and group usage information in *ZFS user/group used.*

At *DSL deadlist map*, we see the dead list of blocks removed after the last snapshot has been taken. The dead list uses 244 blocks, or 315 KB.

The *deferred free* line shows how many blocks are scheduled to be released, but haven't been yet.

Finally, there's an *other* line. Because every accounting system requires an "other" bucket.

ZFS Configuration

You can view the system's ZFS configuration with `zdb -C`. If you add the name of a pool, zdb pulls the information from the pool. If you skip the pool, zdb(8) displays everything from *zpool.cache*.

```
# zdb -C media
MOS Configuration:
 version: 5000
 name: 'media'
 state: 0
 txg: 15612202
 pool_guid: 16862785426161824963
 hostid: 2655503804
 hostname: ''
 vdev_children: 1
 vdev_tree:
  type: 'root'
  id: 0
  guid: 16862785426161824963
  create_txg: 4
```

This gives basic detail for the pool *media*. Some of this information is fairly obvious, such as the pool's GUID and the hostid if the host using this pool. This pool has had 15,612,202 transaction groups committed to it. The *vdev_children* field shows how many VDEVs are part of this pool.

Pool VDEV information is displayed as a tree, listing each VDEV and then the disks in that VDEV. Here's a VDEV in the *media* pool.

```
children[0]:
 type: 'raidz'
 id: 0
 guid: 8519167489302904218
 nparity: 2
 metaslab_array: 30
 metaslab_shift: 37
 ashift: 12
 asize: 17990635487232
 is_log: 0
 create_txg: 4
```

You remember specifying an **ashift** when creating a VDEV? Here's where you find out what that was. You'll also see the VDEV's GUID and VDEV type, as well as details on other ZFS internals.

Each disk in the VDEV also gets an entry.

```
children[0]:
 type: 'disk'
 id: 0
 guid: 14921375587032757624
 path: '/dev/ada1p3'
 phys_path: '/dev/ada1p3'
 whole_disk: 1
 DTL: 8495
 create_txg: 4
```

This tells you about the ZFS GUID, the FreeBSD device node, and some internals.

At the very bottom, you'll see a list of read-only features on this pool.

```
features_for_read:
  com.delphix:hole_birth
  com.delphix:embedded_data
```

If you use a second `-C` along with a pool name, `zdb` retrieves both the on-disk and the cached data so you can compare them. Should these differ? Not really.

Dataset Information

Examining a dataset in detail can also provide a lot of information, and help visualize the internals of the filesystem.

Dataset Basics

To see a dataset's basic internal information, use `-d` and the dataset name. Here we examine a dataset on the *media* pool used in the previous section.

```
# zdb -d media/svn/base
Dataset media/svn/base [ZPL], ID 4778, cr_txg 4820082,
3.82G, 259339 objects
```

That did not provide very much information. The *cr_txg* field shows the transaction group where this dataset was created, number 4,820,082 of 15,612,202 on this pool. It holds 3.82 GB worth of data, and has 259,339 objects in it. Objects include files and directories, but also metadata, ACLs, and every other type of data ZFS can hold.

Dataset Detail

You want more detail? You got it. Add a second `-d` and hang on to your hat. You might want to run this under script(1) or another terminal recording program.

```
# zdb -dd media/svn/base
Dataset media/svn/base [ZPL], ID 4778, cr_txg 4820082, 3.82G, 259339
objects
  Object  lvl   iblk   dblk  dsize  lsize   %full  type
       0    7    16K    16K   417M   632M   20.04  DMU dnode
      -1    1    16K     1K      0     1K  100.00  ZFS user/group used
      -2    1    16K     1K      0     1K  100.00  ZFS user/group used
       1    1    16K     1K    16K     1K  100.00  ZFS master node
       2    1    16K    512    16K    512  100.00  SA master node
...
       9    1    16K  16.5K    16K  16.5K  100.00  ZFS directory
      11    3    16K   128K  43.3M   155M   82.49  ZFS plain file
      13    1    16K    512     8K    512  100.00  ZFS plain file
...
```

How long does this go on? Well…

```
 1294291    1    16K  3.50K     8K  3.50K  100.00  ZFS plain file
 1294324    1    16K     4K     8K     4K  100.00  ZFS plain file
 1294328    1    16K  4.50K     8K  4.50K  100.00  ZFS plain file
```

This dataset has a whole bunch of files, directories, and related stuff in it.

A few of the columns might be of interest to sysadmins. The first column is the object number. The *dblk* column is the record size used for this object. The *lsize* is the logical size of the object, what most of us think of when we say "file size."

The first line gives us the basic information. After that, though, we see details on every object on the dataset. While the first few objects are always ZFS metadata, later objects are mostly files and directories. You'll see the values assigned to the object's data structures.

Examining Specific Objects

This list of dataset objects might have its interest, but what is each of those objects? Examine an object by specifying its object number after the dataset name. Here, we turn `zdb` all the way up, and investigate object 1,294,328 on the *media/svn/base* dataset.

```
# zdb -ddddd media/svn/base 1294328
Dataset media/svn/base [ZPL], ID 4778, cr_
txg 4820082, 3.82G, 259339 objects, rootbp
DVA[0]=<0:bc346503000:3000> DVA[1]=<0:f005fc91000:3000>
[L0 DMU objset] fletcher4 uncompressed LE contiguous
unique double size=800L/800P birth=15618812L/15618812P
fill=259339 cksum=1003e8933c:10304c47fe66:af75e77a47ed-
d:5dcc1d2be9f01d9
```

We start with details about the dataset, such as the creation txg and number of objects, exactly as we saw on less intensive `zdb` queries. We also get a bunch more details, such as the current checksums and other things that only make sense if you're studying *D&I*.

Then we get some detail on the file itself.

```
 Object  lvl  iblk   dblk  dsize  lsize   %full  type
1294328    1   16K  4.50K     8K  4.50K  100.00  ZFS plain file
                                     168   bonus  System attributes
```

This file is 4.50 KB in size, but the data size (*dsize*) is 8 KB because the on-disk size is in whole sectors.

We'll then get into the guts of the file.

```
    dnode flags: USED_BYTES USERUSED_ACCOUNTED
    dnode maxblkid: 0
    path  /head/sys/arm64/include/bus_dma_impl.h
    uid   1001
    gid   1001
    atime   Sat May  9 12:40:22 2015
    mtime   Sat May  9 12:40:22 2015
    ctime   Sat May  9 12:40:22 2015
    crtime  Sat May  9 12:40:22 2015
    gen   10832525
    mode  100644
    size  4139
    parent  1247454
    links   1
    pflags  40800000004
Indirect blocks:
            0 L0 0:e1c09620000:3000 1200L/a00P F=1 B=10832525/10832525
             segment [0000000000000000, 0000000000001200) size 4.50K
```

You'll see a bunch of traditional Unix information: permissions, file name and path, timing, parent object, and more. If you look at this file with ls(1) the file appears to be 4,139 bytes, but that doesn't include any of the ZFS metadata that supports it.

Now let's consider a larger, lz4-compressed file.

```
# zdb -ddddd zstore/tmp 3628
...
 Object  lvl  iblk  dblk  dsize  lsize   %full  type
   3628    2   16K  128K   244K   896K  100.00  ZFS plain file
                                    168   bonus  System attributes
```

This starts with basic pool information, but then dives into the file itself. While this file takes 244 KB of disk space, its true size is 896 KB. Compression reduces the amount of disk space needed.

After the Unix information, though, we get a list of indirect blocks.

```
Indirect blocks:
       0  L1 0:20edc2ec000:2000  4000L/1000P F=7 B=15965896/15965896
       0  L0 0:188fc2c8000:c000 20000L/8000P F=1 B=15965895/15965895
   20000  L0 0:188fc2f8000:c000 20000L/8000P F=1 B=15965895/15965895
   40000  L0 0:188fc2ec000:c000 20000L/8000P F=1 B=15965895/15965895
   60000  L0 0:188fc2e0000:c000 20000L/8000P F=1 B=15965895/15965895
   80000  L0 0:188fc2d4000:c000 20000L/8000P F=1 B=15965895/15965895
   a0000  L0 0:188fc324000:c000 20000L/8000P F=1 B=15965895/15965895
   c0000  L0 0:20834cea000:8000 20000L/6000P F=1 B=15965896/15965896

    segment [0000000000000000, 00000000000e0000) size  896K
```

When a file is larger than the recordsize (*dblk*), ZFS stores it as multiple separate blocks. The first column is the offset in the file, in hex. The number 20,000 in hex is 128 KB. The file in question has an L1 indirect block, and then seven 128 KB L0 blocks that actually hold the data, the last of which is actually slightly smaller.

Examining Specific Files

Maybe you want to look at a particular file—say, to see what block size it was written with. You can't easily extract that from `zdb -d`, but you can get a serial or inode number from ls(1) by using the `-i` flag. Here, for some unspeakable reason, we're interested in a MySQL data file.

```
# ls -i /var/mysql/nyaargh/users.MYI
132 /var/mysql/nyaargh/users.MYI
```

This is file 132 on the *zroot/var/mysql* dataset.

When you're working from an inode number, use the `-v` flag to zdb(8).

```
# zdb -v zroot/var/mysql 132
Dataset zroot/var/mysql [ZPL], ID 128, cr_txg 18594, 293M, 534 objects

    Object  lvl   iblk   dblk  dsize  lsize   %full  type
       132    1    16K  6.00K     8K  6.00K  100.00  ZFS plain file
```

Using four or more `-v` flags displays the traditional Unix information and the indirect blocks. If you have ls(1), you probably have the traditional Unix information already.

Metaslabs and Free Space Histograms

Each top-level virtual device is broken up into *metaslabs*. ZFS fills space on a metaslab-by-metaslab basis.

When ZFS allocates space, it looks for chunks of disk big enough to hold the new transaction. When your pool gets full, your only option when writing data is to break it up into these small chunks of space that are left. This is why ZFS performance decreases as the pool fills—the free space becomes fragmented. See how full your metaslabs are by viewing metaslab histograms.

```
# zdb -mmm media
Metaslabs:
      vdev         0
      metaslabs  130   offset            spacemap          free
      ---------------  ---------------   ---------------   -----------
      metaslab     0   offset        0   spacemap   8317   free  4.72G
                       segments    806   maxsize   4.68G   freepct  3%
```

Each metaslab definition starts with a basic description. Here we're looking at VDEV 0, which has 130 metaslabs. We then proceed to metaslab number 0. It's right at the beginning of the pool, with an offset of 0. This pool has 806 allocations, or segments. Only three percent of them are free.

We then get a histogram of how blocks in this metaslab are allocated, as far as the system memory is concerned.

```
In-memory histogram:
   13:  281 ****************************************
   14:  197 *****************************
   15:  189 ***************************
   16:  106 ****************
   17:   27 ****
   18:    5 *
   19:    0
   20:    0
...
   31:    0
   32:    1 *
```

The numbers in the first column are block sizes, shown as kilobytes in powers of 2. $2^{13} = 8,192$, so 13 is 8 KB. This metaslab has 281 8 KB allocations.

Line 14 is 16 KB. This metaslab has 197 16 KB allocations.

Line 15 is 32 KB, with 189 allocations, and so on, all the way up to a single 2^{32} (or 4 GB) allocation.

After the histogram of the metaslab in memory, we get to see how the version of the metaslab on the disk looks. On a busy disk, ZFS is always allocating and de-allocating blocks.

```
On-disk histogram:              fragmentation 0
   13:  295 ****************************************
   14:  198 ***************************
   15:  189 **************************
   16:  107 ***************
   17:   29 ****
   18:    3 *
...
   32:    1 *
```

Scroll down. No, further. Eventually, you'll come to a later metaslab that looks considerably different. Metaslab 43, in this case.

```
metaslab    43   offset  56000000000  spacemap  8280  free  59.1G
                 segments      17893  maxsize   815M  freepct   46%
```

This metaslab has 17,893 allocations, but is 46 percent free. And the block size distribution is considerably different.

```
In-memory histogram:
   13:    891 *********
   14:    565 ******
   15:    806 ********
   16:    994 **********
   17:   3341 *******************************
   18:   1452 **************
   19:   1932 ******************
   20:   4406 ****************************************
   21:   1557 ***************
   22:    934 *********
   23:    488 *****
   24:    272 ***
   25:    103 *
   26:     80 *
   27:     47 *
   28:     19 *
   29:      6 *
```

Our most common allocations are 17 (128 KB) and 20 (1 MB).

The disk gives a hint why this metaslab is only about half full, though.

```
     On-disk histogram:              fragmentation 11
    13:    7520 ***********************
    14:    5702 ******************
    15:    4096 *************
...
```

Note the fragmentation level—11. On the disk, metaslab 43 is fragmented. This means that many of the chunks of free space are relatively small. With spinning disks, storing chunks of a file contiguously improves performance. If ZFS needs to write a large block, it'll probably proceed to a later metaslab.

Descend even further down into the bowels of your metaslabs.

```
metaslab  121  offset  f2000000000  spacemap    0  free
128G
               segments            1  maxsize  128G
freepct  100%
In-memory histogram:
    37:    1 *
```

The metaslabs near the end of the disk are made up of contiguous 128 GB chunks. If this pool had previously been nearly full, the higher-numbered metaslabs would likely contain bits of data, whereas on this pool, they are untouched.

ZFS normally divides a VDEV up into 200 metaslabs of equal size. You can tune this number with the vfs.zfs.vdev.metaslabs_per_vdev sysctl, but you must set the sysctl before creating the VDEV. The number 200 was chosen because it seemed to work pretty well, but there's lots of room for experimenting with metaslab allocations.

When you expand a VDEV by replacing its disks with larger ones, ZFS creates new metaslabs to support the increased space. You can get a pool with far more than 200 metaslabs this way.

ZFS can only keep so many metaslabs in memory at once. Growing a VDEV to many times its original size can have a negative performance impact, as ZFS shuffles metaslabs to and from disk.

Uberblock

What kind of ZFS debugging section would this be without taking a look at pool's uberblock?

```
# zdb -u media
Uberblock:
  magic = 0000000000bab10c
  version = 5000
  txg = 15741196
  guid_sum = 7884957152936881795
  timestamp = 1456030423 UTC = Sat Feb 20 23:53:43 2016
```

What can you do with this? Not much. But at this point, ZFS pretty much lies naked and exposed before you.

What else you learn is up to you.

Afterword

Allan has gone off to AsiaBSDCon 2016, leaving me to write the afterword on my own.

Many tools change how we practice systems administration. ZFS is practically unique, in that the change is for the better. Once you've used ZFS for a while, other filesystems seem positively quaint. I administered various iterations of UFS and EXT for two decades, but after only a few months of using ZFS, the inability to do a `ufs send` or `ufs clone` would instantly drive me to a red rage. Fortunately, UFS does have snapshots, so I was able to regain my composure before too many people got permanently maimed.

What's more, this is the last of four books on FreeBSD storage. I'd like to note that, at long last, I've written a tetralogy. Well, most of a tetralogy. Yeah, without Allan's help some of this stuff wouldn't have been in here—Allan knows more than I do, and he gave both ZFS books a depth I couldn't have alone. And he has hardware I don't, like multipath SAS, meaning he could write those sections when I simply couldn't. And he knew who to ask to get access to hardware neither of us owned, like NVMe. Yeah, fine, without Allan my tetralogy would have been a trilogy, and the single ZFS volume would not have been nearly as good—but that's not my point. What is my point? Oh, look—over there! A man-eating platypus! Run away!

Sponsors

The following fine folks thought that this book was important enough that they offered Lucas financial support as he produced it. Ebook sponsors paid at least $20 for the privilege of getting their name in the electronic version, while the maniacs who sponsored the print version shelled out at least $100 to get their name immortalized on that edition's soft, absorbent pages.

Four days after sponsorships went on sale, Lucas' hot water heater died. In February. In Michigan. Those initial sponsors almost exactly covered the cost of the water heater.

Thank you all. Very much.

Dan Langille
TransIP B.V.
Andy Scott
Dirk Tol
Justin D Holcomb, in memory of Mary Lou Malott
Adam McDougall
Miguel Moll
Dominik B. Kowal
Lex Onderwater
Alexandre Peyroux pour Angélique, Emma et Thybalt Peyroux
Adrian Jaskuła

About the Authors

Allan Jude is VP of operations at ScaleEngine Inc., a global Video Streaming CDN, where he makes extensive use of ZFS on FreeBSD.

He is also the host of the weekly video podcasts BSD Now (with Kris Moore) and TechSNAP on JupiterBroadcasting.com. Allan is a FreeBSD committer, focused on improving the documention and implementing libucl and libxo throughout the base system. He taught FreeBSD and NetBSD at Mohawk College in Hamilton, Canada from 2007-2010 and has 13 years of BSD unix sysadmin experience.

Michael W Lucas is a full time author. His FreeBSD experience is almost as old as FreeBSD. He worked for twenty years as a sysadmin

and network engineer at a variety of firms, most of which no longer exist. He's written a whole stack of technology books, which have been translated into nine languages. (Yes, real languages. Ones that people actually speak.) You can find him lurking at various user groups around Detroit, Michigan, his dojo (http://zenmartialarts.com), or at https://www.michaelwlucas.com.

Find the authors on Twitter as @allanjude and @mwlauthor.

Never miss a new Lucas release!

Sign up for Michael W Lucas' mailing list.
https://mwl.io

More Tech Books from Michael W Lucas

Absolute BSD
Absolute OpenBSD (1st and 2nd edition)
Cisco Routers for the Desperate (1st and 2nd edition)
PGP and GPG
Absolute FreeBSD
Network Flow Analysis
Absolute FreeBSD 3rd edition (coming 2018)

the IT Mastery Series

SSH Mastery
DNSSEC Mastery
Sudo Mastery
FreeBSD Mastery: Storage Essentials
Networking for Systems Administrators
Tarsnap Mastery
FreeBSD Mastery: ZFS
FreeBSD Mastery: Specialty Filesystems
FreeBSD Mastery: Advanced ZFS
PAM Mastery
Relayd and Httpd Mastery
SSH Mastery 2nd edition (coming 2018)

Novels (as Michael Warren Lucas)

git commit murder
git sync murder (coming 2018)
Immortal Clay
Kipuka Blues
Bones Like Water (coming 2018)
Butterfly Stomp Waltz
Hydrogen Sleets

13397063R00139

Printed in Germany
by Amazon Distribution
GmbH, Leipzig